If you love somebody who smokes

Confessions of a nicotine addict

by
Cynthia Morgan

City Miner ⚒ *Books*

Published by City Miner Books
P.O. Box 176, Berkeley, California 94701

Cover photo provided by Underwood Photo Archives
Cover Design by Joan Rhine
Book Design and Typesetting by Harrington-Young
Typeset in Plantin
Printed by McNaughton & Gunn

Library of Congress Card Catalogue Number: 87-071061
ISBN: 0-933944-14-4

10 9 8 7 6 5 4 3 2 1 0

*This book is dedicated to my daughter, Sybil,
without whom it probably would never
have been written.*

Table of Contents

1 Me, Myself and My Addiction

"You're absolutely addicted to smoking. You'll never quit."
"That's ridiculous! I've quit hundreds of times!"

MARK TWAIN

There are no limits to the depths I have sunk for a cigarette. Walk a mile for a Camel? I would have hopped it on a pogo stick. The cigarette has humbled me. I was one of those people who could talk all evening about quitting (boring everyone else in the room) then get the CRAVING and end up out in the street looking for butts in the ashtrays of my friends' cars. I have looked for butts in gutters, bummed cigarettes off strangers.

There has been a veil of smoke in my corner of the world. I have missed the best parts of movies while getting my fix out in the lobby. During *Raiders of the Lost Ark,* I missed the snake pit scene. When I came back from the lobby during *Dr. Zhivago* I couldn't figure out why Omar Sharif was suddenly living with Julie Christie instead of his wife. I am probably the only person watching *The Terminator* who tore herself away for a smoke. In the lobbies of theatres, when I was out of smokes, my fingers have sifted through sand-filled ashtrays groping blindly for the longest butts. For all I knew the mouths previously caressing these butts could have had halitosis, herpes, a bloody root canal that very afternoon. The people behind those mouths might have been murderers, paranoid schizophrenics on valium, members of the Ku Klux Klan. They could have been anyone— the Zodiac Killer, Lee Harvey Oswald. My only disease precaution was, "Well, if they paid to see this movie, they can't be *all* bad."

Upon my life's path I have left a trail of ash. I have traveled twenty miles down a slippery mountain road at 1:00 a.m. in rain and hail, skidding through mud slides, small boulders tapping the roof of my car, all for a pack of cigarettes.

I have set a small portion of the world on fire. Burned tiny round holes in the fronts of a dozen blouses and singed hundreds of stockings.

Cigarettes seduced me before any lover and have remained with me longer. I remember the day I smoked my first one. I was ten years old. I stayed home from school because I didn't want to take a test. Late in the morning my mother went to the grocery store to get some Squirt and 7 Up for my fictionalized stomach ache. She left me alone, propped up against two pillows in the den on the couch watching "Queen For A Day." A harmless enough scene except for my father's pack of Winstons on top of the television.

I don't know what possessed me to light one. I hated the smell of the obnoxious tobacco my father smoked both in the house and in the car. Still, just as the typical American housewife was being crowned queen for a day on TV, I became the typical kid grown up for a day. I lit one. Puff puff. Then, while Jack Bailey handed *her* two dozen long-stemmed red roses, I pretended I was at a cocktail party talking to a doctor and his wife.

"Hello! puff puff. We own the house up on the hill! Puff

puff. You simply must come up sometime for . . . a cigarette!"

As Jack Bailey gave *her* a washer-dryer combo, I gave myself a Rolls Royce. "What does my husband do? He . . . puff puff . . . he's a dentist! We drive a Rolls Royce and we have . . . puff . . . puff . . . three, no—two, children."

She got a dining room set. I got a mansion and a swimming pool. This went on until I heard the squeaky brakes of my mother's olive and yellow Ford station wagon pull into the driveway.

I ran into the bathroom, threw the burning butt in the toilet, flushed it. The car door slammed shut. Click of heels on sidewalk, rustle of grocery bag, rattle of keys . . . by the time the front door opened I was safely back under the blanket watching TV again. The grocery bag hit the kitchen counter. I stuck the thermometer in my mouth.

She stood in the doorway to the den sniffing the air.

"Who's been smoking a cigarette?"

The smell! I hadn't thought of that. "A salesman!" I said.

Sniff sniff. "There was a salesman here while I was gone?"

"Uh huh." "Truth or Consequences" was now coming on the air.

"What was he selling? Cigarettes?"

"Uh . . . vacuums and brushes."

She stood there weighing the possibilities—who had smoked this cigarette, me or the salesman? "Well, what did he do? Just take one out and light it? Did he sit here and . . . ha . . . watch TV with you?"

"He said, 'Do you mind if I smoke a cigarette while I wait for your mother? and I said, 'Go ahead. My father smokes too.'"

"Well, where *is* he then?"

"He left."

At this point her eyes began darting between me and the pack of Winstons on the TV set. I panicked. Did she know how many cigarettes were in the pack? Had this been a test? Should I change my story and tell her I *offered* the salesman one?

"Where's the ashtray? He *did* use an ashtray, didn't he?"

"Ashtray?" I hadn't thought of that one either. "He . . . put it out in the toilet."

After this I don't recall ever seeing a pack of Winstons hanging around the house unless they were sitting next to my father. My first cigarette was tainted more by lying (and enjoying it) than the smoking which wasn't enough to get me hooked.

As for my father, he died at the age of fifty-eight of a heart attack.

2 *The Girl Who Got Me Hooked*

*I*t was my second cigarette that hooked me. If there is a special room in hell for all the people who got other people hooked on smoking cigarettes, that is where Nancy Henderson will end up.

She was three years older than the rest of us on the block, but only a year ahead in school. Her mother was divorced and worked all day. Nancy got to do whatever she wanted and what she wanted to do was eat a lot of Oreo cookies and smoke Salem cigarettes.

One Friday I stayed overnight at her house. We were in her double bed watching TV, drinking Dr. Peppers and munching Oreo cookies (stacked a foot high on her side of the bed). When she whipped the Salems from her purse and slipped the matches out from between the cellophane and the package, I was shocked. Her mother was home! I could hear her mother's TV—"The Hit Parade"—through the wall separating the two bedrooms.

"But your mom's home!" I said.

"So what?" She said.

"Aren't you afraid she'll find out what you're doing?"

"She doesn't care!"

With a whoop and a hurrah, freedom called me forth. This was the first truly democratic household I had ever been in. Now her mother became a sanctioning presence in the next room (although I hadn't even seen her that evening. As a matter of fact I had never seen her. For all I knew, Nancy just *wanted* me to think her mother was home and had turned the TV on herself before I got there).

I watched as Nancy took long draws on her Salem and as she French-inhaled. So worldly! She blew eight doughnut-like smoke rings in front of us. A pro at seventeen!

On TV Bette Davis was also smoking. She had just been told that she was going blind. Upon receiving this unfortunate piece of news the first thing she did was take a cigarette out of a silver case and tap it on the case five times—as if it were a call for help in Morse Code.

tap tap tap—tap tap

After she stuck the cigarette delicately between her parted lips and the *doctor* lit it for her, she smoked it as if this was her last hope to keep from going blind.

The two of them were making it look like such an amusing sport that I put one of the Salems into my mouth and lit it. Now all three of us were smoking and the room was so thick with smoke we could barely see each other.

But I wasn't really smoking. I was just taking it into my mouth and blowing it out. I wasn't yet taking it in *all the way.* Nancy spent the rest of the evening teaching me how to draw the smoke deep into my lungs. She taught me how to French inhale. It was fun. For the next week or two, like any decent dope peddler, Nancy let me smoke as many of her Salems as I wanted. After that I was on my own.

Sometimes I wonder what ever became of Nancy. She probably got married and then divorced and is living in a trailer park with two kids outside Las Vegas.

3 The First
Tobacco Peddlers

*A*s far as we know tobacco smoking originated among the
Mayans whose civilization began sometime around the
birth of Christ. Stone carvings found in the coastal areas of
Central America and Mexico depict Mayan priests blowing
tobacco smoke out of a pipe toward the sun and the four points
of the globe. Tobacco progressed northward among native cultures and was used principally in religious ceremonies. In
Mexico the Aztecs used reeds for tobacco pipes. Under the
burial mounds in the Mississippi Basin archaeologists have
unearthed pipes of fantastic design made of clay, bone and wood
which may be over 1,500 years old.

It may have been the wishful thinking of those early
priests (our first nicotine addicts?) which created the notion that
to the gods the smell of tobacco was sweet. Many of the religious
rites and customs of these Indians sprang out of the belief that
smoke, through the mystery of fire, disappeared into a crack in
the void of nothingness where they believed the gods lived.

The American natives believed smoke calmed the waters
and lured fish into their nets. The peace pipe was used ritu-
alistically to enhance good will. Among the Indians there
doesn't seem to be any concern that smoking was bad for them.

Having the sanction of the priests it was used by medicine men as a remedial and by your average Indian to assuage respiratory illnesses. They were so devoted to the pipe they used it like a watch, saying to themselves, "I was one pipe about it."

Sailors that rode the ships between America and Spain were Europe's first smokers. When Columbus landed in the New World in 1492, the natives offered him food, drink and a handful of tobacco leaves. He ate the first, reserved some of the liquor to show Queen Isabella and threw away the tobacco. (I wonder, did he just let the tobacco leaves fall from his hands right there in front of the Indians as if they had made some kind of mistake? Or, did he wait tactfully until the Indians were out of sight and then throw them into a bush?) Later on the Indians showed him what they did with the leaves by smoking them in long pipes. He liked it. Tobacco had a place on the boat home to Spain.

Columbus was probably no more surprised at sighting land than he was to see the Indians "drinking" the smoke and pouring it back out their nostrils. It is clear from the diaries of Columbus and his men that the Indians relied heavily upon tobacco. Bartolome Las Casas wrote in his diary on November 5, 1492, ". . . met with great multitudes of people, men and women, with firebrands in their hands and herbs to smoke after their custom."

During the same voyage, on Monday, October 25, Columbus wrote, ". . . being at sea, about midway between Santa Maria and the large island, which I name Fernandina, we met a man in a canoe going from Santa Maria. . . . He had with him a piece of bread which the natives make, as big as one's fist, a calabash of water, a quantity of reddish earth, pulverized and afterwards kneaded up, and some dried leaves which are in high value among them, for a quantity of it was brought to me at San Salvador. . . ."[1]

The monk, Romano Pane, took notes while sailing on the second voyage with Columbus. He described the Indians both smoking the herb and snuffing it in powder form. It was only when tobacco hit Europe that the two habits took separate paths. Most countries took to snuff as a form of pleasure while smoking the tobacco only for medicinal purposes.

In 1559 Jean Nicot, a French ambassador at Lisbon, acquainted his country with tobacco. Nicot got slips of the plant and grew tobacco in his garden at home. He not only healed ringworm, ulcers and cancers thought to be incurable, but saved his cook who had cut off "almost all of his thombe . . . with a great kitchen knife."[2] Because so many came to him to be healed and he encouraged the development of a new era in medical science, it is Nicot's name that graces the botanical plant as *Nicotannia.*

Many people took tobacco as a preventative against infection during the Great Plague in 1665. School children were forced to smoke in their classrooms and were whipped if they didn't.[3] Those who tended the sick and carted corpses out of the city smoked incessantly. Samuel Pepys wrote in his diary on June 7, 1665, ". . . the hottest day that ever I felt in my life. This day, much against my will, I did in Drury Lane see two or three houses marked with a red cross upon the doors and 'Lord, have mercy upon us!' writ there; which was a sad sight to me. . . . I was forced to buy some roll tobacco to smell and chew, which took away the apprehension."[4]

By the middle of the seventeenth century European seamen had introduced smoking to every continent in the world except Australia. Compared to the rest of Europe, smoking in England took a decadent form. It has been reported that one stormy night both Ben Jonson and Shakespeare were drinking at the Mermaid Tavern when Sir Walter Raleigh threw some tobacco, along with several pipes, onto their table and beckoned them to smoke. Shakespeare thought smoke more appropriate for Hell and suggested his rival, Sir Francis Bacon, be given the monopoly of it. It is not known (as so much is not known about him) whether or not Shakespeare ever took to smoking. We can only go by hints such as the one Ben Johnson dropped when he said, "Tobacco, I do assert without fear of contradiction from the Avon skylark (i.e., Shakespeare), is the most soothing, sovereign, and precious weed that ever our dear old Mother Earth tendered to the use of men."[5]

There are many amusing stories written about Sir Walter Raleigh and tobacco. In 1708 a magazine called *The British Apollo* ran a story in which Sir Walter Raleigh's servant brought him his evening tankard of old ale and nutmeg, saw his master smoking for the first time, and doused the fire out with his own drink. Raleigh once wagered Queen Elizabeth he could weigh smoke. He put a pipeful on a scale, weighed and then smoked it. Afterwards he knocked the ash out onto the scale and weighed *that*. The difference, he said, had gone up in smoke. After she lost the bet, Queen Elizabeth said, "Many alchemists have I heard of who turned gold into smoke, but Raleigh is the first who turned smoke into gold."[6]

If Sir James Barrie is correct, the English Renaissance may owe its very existence to tobacco. To quote from his *My Lady Nicotine*, "I know, I feel, that with the introduction of tobacco England woke up from a long sleep. . . . The glory of existence became a thing to speak of. Men who had hitherto only concerned themselves with the narrow things of home put a pipe into their mouths and became philosophers."[7]

Any night at the Mermaid Tavern the famous writers of the day could be seen smoking their pipes. In general the coffee rooms reeked with tobacco and strangers sometimes expressed their surprise that so many people should leave their own firesides to sit in the midst of "fogge" and "stinke."

Since tobacco was an expensive pleasure, sold then for its weight in silver, the poor took to it slowly. Clay pipes were passed around their taverns. Those who couldn't afford to go to a tavern, the poorest of the poor, scavenged their tobacco, which they smoked out of pipes made from walnut shells with straw stems. Contrary to popular opinion, the first cigarette was conceived not in a vending machine but in a garbage can. The first cigarette was born fat, like a cigar. Beggars in cities would search through the garbage seeking food, discards and those things one could sell at flea markets. One day (we'll call it Cigarettmas) they came upon cigar butts, snuff dust and pipe dottle. These they mixed into the first blend and rolled into "mini" cigars which soon came to be called "cigarellos." Several peasants would stand huddled over the garbage sharing a cigarello the same way tramps today share a bottle of sweet wine.

Meanwhile the English aristocrats took their tobacco and boxes of assorted silver pipes to the theater. It is said that this was legitimized after Christopher Marlowe smoked at one of his own plays, perhaps *Dr. Faustus*? At the Elizabethan plays, where Shakespeare was in full swing by now, these "reeking gallants," as they were called, would sit at the side of the stage clouding the air with the loathed fog and fume while heckling the actors. It is easy to imagine their antics rivaling the comedy taking place on the stage. To amuse themselves and others, they learned how to perform smoking tricks such as "The Ring," "The Whiffe," "The Gulp," and "The Retention." While they performed they had their regalia spread out all around them—a set of Winchester clays, teak and silver boxes with mirrors on the inside of the lid so they could gaze at their handsome selves. These boxes contained up to a pound of tobacco, a pick and knife to shred the tobacco and silver tongs for lifting a glowing ember to light one's pipe. Serving boys supplied matches by passing the burning tip of a gilt-handled sword from one reeking gallant to another.[8]

Ironically, it was the French Revolution that gave cigarettes a boost into the world by changing the habits of European society. Out of fashion now were wigs, frilly clothes, elaborate pipes and snuff snorting. For sake of appearances frightened aristocrats purchased short peasant pipes and "cigarellos" which suggested sympathy with the lower classes. Eventually the defeat of Napoleon (who would not smoke because it made him gag) caused the popularity of cigarellos to dwindle. Except among artists, writers and others who remained true to the revolutionary cause of, uh, freedom.

This immense joke holds true today wherever bohemians gather. It remains an enigma why freedom is still associated with being able to take smoke into your lungs.

4 Confessions of a Teenage Smoker

Once Nancy had gotten all the teenage girls in my neighborhood hooked we begged, borrowed and stole our cigarette money. We squandered our babysitting money and allowances on them. We marched through the plum orchard to the Shell gas station in squadrons with the change jangling in our pockets. We slipped our quarters into the slot of the vending machine and grinned sheepishly while we watched the green packs of Salems (we had yet to show independence in our choice of brands) slide down the chute. Once the packs were in our pockets we walked back to the orchard and sat under the trees smoking and talking about boys. Judy Heron was the only holdout. Her pockets bulged with nickel packs of David's sunflower seeds which she cracked between her teeth every ten seconds.

When I was fourteen I kept my cigarettes hidden outside under a rock. By age fifteen I hid them under my mattress. At sixteen they were in my top bureau drawer with my underwear. When I was seventeen I was carrying them in my purse.

In 1963 cigarettes were twenty-five cents a pack and gasoline was twenty-five cents a gallon. For a mere seventy-five cents I could drive over the hill from Sunnyvale to Santa Cruz and spend the day smoking on the beach with my friends. For the ride they would pitch in and buy my lunch. Pretty good deal.

But smoking wasn't just a bed of roses. If a pack of cigarettes hadn't sent me to jail when I was a teenager my life's path might not have gone so crooked.

It all began simply enough: 1. My parents went to San Francisco one weekend. 2. I threw a party at our house while they were gone. 3. Some of my girlfriends called the local radio station KLIV and not only told the D.J. about the party but gave him the address. 4. This information was put on the air. At that point my party was no longer a party—it was an "event."

People I had never seen before showed up. Soon I was outside helping the troops of cops the neighbors had called re-route the scores of low riders in '55 Chevys and football players in Continentals to distant shores. Meanwhile, all my friends were having a good ol' time inside my house listening to my 45's, drinking beer and smoking. Even from the street I could see the cigarette smoke pouring out the windows.

Somewhere around 11:00 p.m. the cops raided the party a second time. After about eighty people had been booted out one of the cops asked me, "Where are your parents?"

I told him they were in San Francisco. (It is a big city. The cops would never find them.)

"Do they know you're having a party?"

"Yes." I lied.

We were standing in the living room at the time, a dozen or so people were loitering.

"What would you do if there was a fire?"

I was about to answer (the *correct* answer), "Call the Fire Department," when Larry Pascal, my brother's best friend, answered for me in his usual sarcastic tone . . . "Call the Fire Department!"

The cop turned and slugged him.

"That could have been me," I thought. And then I tried to guess the right answer—If there is a fire you call . . . the police? The YMCA? The Red Cross? Later, after the cops left, everyone else who had been in the living room said that they would have given Larry's answer, too. So why was Larry slugged? Had we all missed something? Yes. In our teenage naivete, we didn't realize that with our beer and cigarettes we were all potential fire hazards running willy nilly like a swarm of fireflies around the house. It had been a simple routine question. Larry just hadn't answered it with the proper seriousness.

The next morning we awoke to the reality. There were cigarettes everywhere; in ashtrays, falling out of ashtrays onto tables, on the record cabinet, ground down into the rugs, burned down to filters on the mantle and the bathroom sinks. As it turned out, we *had* caused fires. A lot of little fires.

After my parents returned from their pleasant weekend in the city it was the burn holes in the drapes and living room carpet that got me grounded for three months. Not to mention the butts we couldn't fish out of the swimming pool because they had dissolved and looked like little amber-colored guppies swimming around in the water. We would have had to drain the whole pool to get the tobacco out. And then there was the butt my mother found in one of her high-heeled shoes in her closet where I had hidden four people during the second raid.

This episode was only the first stage in what I call the Cigarette Curse that haunted me throughout the winter of 1963. A month after my party, Dave Robertson gave a party that was to last the duration of our Christmas vacation (*his* parents went to the Bahamas). I was still grounded because of my party so I stuffed my bed every night at 10:00 with pillows and snuck out my window to speed off in an awaiting car to Dave's house. If my parents had looked out the window during a commercial they would not have suspected the getaway car parked across the street unless they had noticed the three, perhaps four, glowing tips of cigarettes my comrades were smoking while they waited for me to break out of the house.

It was late on the eve of December 28th (or was it the

morning of the 29th?) that we ran out of cigarettes while playing poker. Bob Murphey and I took orders and drove to the nearest gas station to make the purchases. I was stacking the cigarettes on top of the vending machine and checking my list . . . "Two packs of Winstons, check; three Marlboros, check; two Salems, check." . . . when a police car came into the station to get gas. The two cops saw me standing by the machine and (considering what happened five minutes later) here is how their conversation probably went:

"Say, isn't she the girl who gave that wild party last month?"

"Yeah, that's her!"

"Isn't she the one who almost burned up her parents' house?"

"Yeah, that's her all right!"

"What kind of trouble do you think she's brewing up tonight?"

"I don't know. Look at all those cigarettes. She sure must like to smoke!"

"Where there's smoke there's fire. I'll bet you tonight's dinner she's on a cigarette run. She's probably at another party."

"She's our raid bait!"

"Let's take our party girl down to the station!"

If I hadn't been a teen smoker I would not have been taken down to the Sunnyvale jail that night. And an hour later neither would the rest of my friends at the party. If I hadn't been a teen smoker my parents would never have gotten that call in the middle of the night.

"My daughter in jail? You must be mistaken, she's in bed. . . . Go check the contents of the bed? All right."

If I hadn't been a teen smoker my father would never have discovered that my bed was stuffed with pillows and my mother wouldn't have hit me over the head with my closet hanger after we got home from the police station.

There is no doubt about it, I should have gone on the lam and let somebody *else* make that cigarette run. Now Dave was grounded for three months and my term had been extended to six.

In college I switched to Kents, the intelligent coed's choice. I really enjoyed smoking in college. It was as if I'd always been searching for just the right place to smoke, the place where smoking would look relevant, important, even necessary. For my habit it was like coming home. How I relished burning the candle at both ends while I studied all night, smoked and popped No Doze. There were some classes where the teacher would let us smoke while he lectured. Especially if *he* smoked. I felt so grown up. I felt like I was a young Simone De Beauvoir at the Sorbonne.

After college I tried to quit many times—never lasting more than a few days. It became routine for me to do this once every few months. One time in particular stands out in my memory.

My sister and I were both in our twenties when we decided we would quit smoking together under the premise that we could guard each other against temptation. We would even compete with each other for success, something we, as sisters, had formed the habit of doing.

Late one night after everyone else had left a party we had given, the two of us found ourselves staring at each other from opposite arm chairs in the living room.

"You go to bed," I told her. "I'll clean up the mess."

"No, no. *You* go to bed. *I'll* clean up," she said.

Neither of us budged from our chair. Finally we started cleaning up together. We picked up the wine glasses. The plates of hors d'oeuvres. We wiped the table tops. While I set the game of Monopoly back into its box she took the ashtrays out to the kitchen. She was dumping one of them into the garbage when I caught her sticking a two-inch butt in her pocket. She felt my pocket and found the butt I'd already taken. After we had a good laugh about this we lit our butts and smoked them. This was the end of trying to quit, that time around.

A couple of years later my sister quit successfully. Her first year, the "year of transition," she smoked blueberry cigars without inhaling them. At least that's what she had us all believe. Just last year she finally confessed she'd been inhaling them. I remember most her self-righteousness, her sitting back in the chair after dinner teeter-tottering the cigar between her fingers like Groucho Marx, waving it like the flag of a country I could never enter. Giving me those condescending "poor weak you" looks across the table where I sat smoking my cigarette. Waiting for my head to turn away from her so she could take the smoke into her lungs. Juggling the non-inhaled smoke with the inhaled.

5 Early Opposition

*W*hen many of us started smoking we didn't know what we were getting into. Our society had perpetuated a myth. An ad man's hoax, or shall we say hex, had been performed on us. But the fact that cigarette smoking is dangerous to health is not a recent discovery.

As soon as tobacco appeared in Europe opposition arose. The first cigarette protesters were the British, probably because they were the first to take up smoking as a widespread pleasure. But many considered smoking a sign of lack of respect for the crown and stable society in general. Ben Jonson had one of his characters in the play, *Everyman in His Humor,* make some observations about "roguish tobacco." It's easy to visualize the characters in the play bantering back and forth with the heckling "reeking gallants." It's surprising that there are no direct references to tobacco in the plays of Shakespeare. He probably wanted to remain in the good graces of King James I, who was a tobacco opponent.

We didn't have to wait until 1978 for the Surgeon General to declare smoking dangerous. King James told us so, way back in 1604 with his famous *Counterblast to Tobacco*: "It is like hell in the very substance of it, for it is a stinking loathesome thing, and so is hell." Perhaps it was King James's dislike of Sir Walter Raleigh that made his outbursts so fanatical. He proclaimed the habit had been acquired from barbarous people, that "smoking gallants" were a social menace and that to foster the tobacco trade was to play into the hands of Spanish enemies.

Disapproval of smoking in England was mild compared to some other countries. If you were a closet smoker in Turkey you would probably have had to sneak twenty miles out into the desert for your puffs. In Turkey smoking was forbidden by the Koran. If you were caught smoking, the pipe was stuck through your nose and you were led through the streets on a mule as an example for everyone else.[1] If you lived in China in 1638 you would have been decapitated and your head exposed on a pike for selling tobacco. In Russia you would have been deported to Siberia and had your upper lip slit with a knife.[2] As a Catholic, you might have been excommunicated by a pope. All of this came to a halt, however, when rulers realized they could tax tobacco imports and exports, thereby increasing their own wealth. King James included.

John Rolfe, one of the early English settlers in Virginia, owned the first English tobacco plantation. His references to tobacco in his writing make it clear that smoking was widely enjoyed. There was one instance, however, where his self-interest seemed to surface when he tried to inhibit others in the community from planting tobacco: "Lest the people should spend too much of their tyme and labor in planting tobacco, known to them to be verie vendible in England, and so neglect their tillage of corn, and fall into want thereof, it is provided for, . . . that no farmer or other, who must maintayne themselves shall plant any tobacco, unless he shall yearely manure, get and maintayne for himself and every man servant two acres of ground with corne, which doing they may plant as much tobacco as they will els all their tobacco shal be forfeite to the colony."[3] He speaks of his fellow colonists as if only they were obsessed with tobacco growing over everything else in the New

World, which leads one to suspect that what he was really after was the assurance of his own tobacco sales.

This may be painting an incomplete picture of Rolfe, however. He was also a bridge between the white man and the Indians. It is likely that he knew the Indians better than most of the settlers because of his plantation and the red man's professional expertise at tobacco growing. Of course it was in his own interests to keep the lines open between the two cultures, and it has been written that his courtship and later marriage to the Indian Princess Pocahontas was a diplomatic move on his part because of recent massacres in the colonies. But a letter he wrote suggests he was a man capable of residing in both the practical and romantic worlds at the same time. In this letter he speaks of Pocahontas as the one, "to whom my hart and best thoughts are, and have bin a long time so entangled, and inthralled in so intricate a labyrinth, that I was ever awearied to unwind myself thereout . . . ."[4]

Nearly three hundred years later there were still conflicting opinions about tobacco. The Commander in Chief of American troops cabled Washington during World War I to tell them tobacco was as indispensable as food. He requested thousands of tons immediately. On the other hand, there was fear that what might be won on the battlefield might go up in smoke. The most depressing problem of the postwar period, warned temperance advocate Clarence True, would be coping with a returning army of nicotine addicts. Thomas Edison believed cigarette paper destroyed brain cells. In a letter to Henry Ford he wrote, "I employ no person who smokes cigarettes."[5]

Despite the tobacco companies' efforts to sell the middle class on the alluring values of cigarettes, smoking them was not considered classy in 1914. Even the news that those who had remained on the Titanic went to their dooms puffing on cigarettes, as advertised by the cigarette companies, didn't help.

6   *Happy Birthday to Me*

*I*t was vanity, the basest motivation, that finally got me to think seriously about quitting. The day I turned thirty-five I looked into the bathroom mirror and was shocked. Who was this hag? Had I reached life's decline overnight? I was collapsing, fading on the vine as fast as the portrait of Dorian Gray. My eyelids were drooping, my mouth looked like a prune with little wrinkles above the lips and I had purple blotches under my eyes.

What is this? You mean smoking affects my *looks*, too?

A pathetic three-year drama, culminating in the macabre, ensued. At first I thought it might be a temporary depression over turning thirty-five. But it refused to go away. Soon my chest started to hurt.

So I joined a health club.

But weight lifting made my heart work even harder.

So I became a strict vegetarian. I drank fresh carrot juice every morning. Cooked tofu and brown rice for dinner. All my vegetables were organic. My cheese was rennetless. Pastries, when I ate them, were made from whole wheat flour and honey. I was still smoking up to twenty cigarettes a day, operating under the premise that if cancer should try to take hold all this good food would attack it. The question was, could food prevent a heart attack? "Well, beets might help," I told myself. This was a shoddy compromise akin to setting a broken arm in jello.

When my chest began hurting so much I knew I could no longer lift weights *and* smoke, I quit the health club. It was at this point I realized the awful truth. I would rather commit suicide than quit smoking.

Suicide: The intentional taking of one's own life. I didn't "want" to commit suicide, but had reached the point where I didn't want to live without cigarettes, either. I decided that if I found out they were killing me I would kill myself first.

I began accommodating suicide into my reality. Preparing myself. At first I called this "facing my mortality." I studied some facts on suicide, such as: Most suicides are between the ages of forty and fifty (I was getting close!). Most women lead in attempted suicides, men in successful suicides (I'd have to be careful). Monday is the most popular day to commit suicide (I'd do it on another day, then. Why die with the mob?). Only one in five suicides leaves a suicide note (I'd already started the rough draft of mine—ten pages so far). Eighty percent of people admit to having "played" with thoughts of suicide (comforting). One hundred thousand people attempt suicide in the U.S. every year, but only twenty thousand succeed (Mostly men, if #2 is correct. Why do men have more to die for? More men smoke than women. Is there any correlation?).

Knowing these facts acclimated me. I was now intimate enough with the idea of suicide so that if I needed to commit it, the shock wouldn't kill me first. What were the chances I'd have to do it? Fifty percent? Higher? If I sound blasé, it's only because I read so much about suicide I began thinking of it as ordinary. Mass suicide for humans, I discovered, is not that abnormal.

In 1,000 A.D., when people were expecting the arrival of the anti-Christ, there were many suicides. Eighteenth century Russia had religious sects whose special aim was suicide. They would kill themselves in shifts. Today this is known as "Russian roulette." After the invasion of Western Europe by the Germans in 1940, there was an epidemic of suicides. Hyperintellectual types mostly (uh oh, like me) who could not defend themselves against the contagious delusion of the world's doom. There are tribes that require old and invalid people to "freely" commit suicide in order not to become a burden to the younger people. Old Eskimos go out in the snow to be frozen to death. In Japan, hari-kari is a self-justification, purification and regaining of lost honor.[1]

What is clear here is that it is usually people who think they're going to die anyway who commit suicide. Like me. Is it the anxiety we can't live with? The mere thought of death?

◆   ◆   ◆

As a rule there aren't too many people who relish the idea of suicide. Two exceptions are the American poets Sylvia Plath and Anne Sexton. They used to meet each other in a bar in New York City where they discussed suicide with the same fervor other poets show when talking about meter and rhyme schemes. Eventually they both committed suicide.

(I wonder, have they met on the other side of life? Do they meet regularly at Cloud 9's Spirits and Brew? Are they now discussing life with the same fervor they once discussed death? Do they cup a hand over their mouths when speaking the words "To be born?" Could they now be daring each other to commit birth?)

◆   ◆   ◆

If my future was looking grim, my present was verging on the ghoulish and I wasn't even dying of anything yet. Late at night I sat (smoking) on the couch visualizing my funeral: Everyone was crying and telling each other what a good writer I would have become if only I'd lived. Making up my own eulogy(ies) is the closest I have come to relishing the thought of suicide. Always the minister gave a picturesque and flattering account of my life.

Soon the dialogues in my head progressed to utilitarian concerns. *How* would I do it? Where would I get the pills? The gun? The rope? The gasoline? (That would be a good clean way. Just go up in a puff of smoke. Nobody would ever have to know. Since suicide is a crime, I wouldn't have to make a criminal's exit. How could I go down in history as a murderer of myself if there wasn't any evidence ?) Then I thought, "Why not go for the creme de la creme of deaths? A heroine's death! I could help the peasants fight in El Salvador and let somebody there do the job for me."

One day it came to me that I could be struck down suddenly. A hole in my lung, a heart attack that left me paralyzed so that I couldn't do it on my own. What if it turned out I wouldn't have time to do it myself? Would it be possible to sneak out of my hospital room and get into the pill room? I'd have to get a key, of course. Would I be able to talk my nurse into helping me? Doubtful. Would my sister help me? No. A friend? Maybe. The thought that I might faint one day and wake up to find tubes in my nose and my body paralyzed began to haunt me. What if I ended up a prisoner in hell?

Here, for the first time, I came upon something worth quitting smoking for. A living nightmare is much worse than suicide. A hell on earth is a fate worse than death. Now at night I visualized myself in a stark white hospital room paralyzed— everything but my brain, that is:

Tick tock goes the clock. Clickity click go the heels up and down the hall outside my door. I hear a voice:

ORDERLY (to nurse): Is room 212 available yet?
NURSE: No, the gal who couldn't quit smoking is still in there.
ORDERLY: Gheez, she's been taking that bed up for two years now. When they gonna pass that euthanasia law? She *is* brain dead, isn't she?
NURSE: The doctors think so.

Later the same day the orderly comes in to wash my floor. Orderly (whistling in between sentences): Well, that's what you get for not having any smarts. Blowed a hole clean through your lungs, huh? Brain all burned up too, huh? (He chuckles.) Oh well, here today, gone tomorrow.

Then I would wish I'd quit smoking.

Still, I didn't quit. After all, it wasn't a sure thing that I'd end up like this. So I kept smoking with the gun–rope–over-dose–car-over-cliff–revolutionary's death alternatives tucked into a corner of my mind.

I watched in morbid fascination the evening Marilyn Monroe's life and death were documented on television. I took notes the way my brother used to while watching "Mr. Wiz-ard"—before he went into his room to try the same thing. This program's significance for me was the fact that it took ninety Nembutals to kill her. Until then I had no idea how many pills I'd have to take to do the job.

"Important to remember," I said, stuffing the information into my brain. There was no doubt about it. I now had my big toe over the line of the living sticking into the nether world of spooks. I was flirting appallingly with hobgoblins and ghosts.

Still, I didn't quit. It took one more thing to happen before I would do that.

Late one evening my daughter climbed up the ladder to my loft and scooted onto my bed. I was resting against three pillows reading and, of course, smoking.

"Mom, you smoke too much lately," she said, as if she had come up in order to express this to me.

"I know," I said.

"You should quit."

"I know."

"What if you get cancer. Michelle's mother has a friend who has lung cancer. Her hair is falling out and she has to wear a wig."

"That's too bad."

"Billy's uncle has to wear a voice box because he's got lung cancer. Whenever he talks, he sounds like a robot. Do you want to sound like a robot, mom?"

"I'd kill myself first." Whoops. Did I say that out loud? What was I doing, bringing out the beast?

"How?"

"How what?"

"How would you kill yourself?"

"Pills, ha ha," said the soul of brevity. The cigarette burning between my fingers felt like a lizard dangling there.

"But what if I come home from school and find you before the pills kill you?"

I wanted to say, "Just pretend you don't see me and go and visit a friend for an hour." But I didn't. I didn't say anything.

And she didn't stop. "I'd have to call an ambulance if I found you like that, mom. And you'd have to get your stomach pumped. Who knows, maybe they'll put a tube in your throat after you get out of the hospital—*if* you get out of the hospital. And if and when you do, everybody will be watching you all the time to make sure you don't try it again and they'll feel sorry for you. Or *worse*. They'll laugh at you and say, 'There goes the lady who tried to commit suicide! I wonder if she feels like committing suicide today? Maybe we should follow her so we can stop her if she tries it again!'"

I found myself thinking, "Well, I'll just have to get it right the first time." Then I played out a wonderful likeness of Blanche Dubois, the crazy sister in *A Streetcar Named Desire*, the one who says, "I've always depended on the kindness of strangers." It went like this:

"Sybil doesn't know I've already weighed all the possibilities. *She* doesn't know I've already decided not to do it at home. Why, I'd never risk her finding me like that! I'll go away . . . to another country, another state . . . I'll do it in a hotel room. I'll do it on Route 66 and wear a pair of red capri pants, bleach my hair so no one will recognize me. Leave a fake suicide note to confuse the computers. Why, if I'm careful, Sybil will never have to know I did it at all. Not if they can't identify the body! She'll just think I went away on a trip! Every year she'll think is the year I'm coming home. Why, this way, instead of telling her children that grandmother was a fool, she'll tell them, 'Grandma went on a trip.' Yes! This is the best of all possible ways!"

(As I look back on this time of my life, I wonder why I never bothered to worry about my sanity going before my lungs or heart. In a way, that would have solved the whole problem.)

"How? *How* are you going to get it right the first time?" she was saying.

It was beginning to sound like a game. So I took two things out of the corner. "I'll use a gun and I'll put a bullet through my head."

"But what if you miss? What if you shoot off half your face and you're still alive? Then you'll have to walk around with only half a face for the rest of your life. The doctors could never put the whole thing back together again." She sang "Humpty Dumpty" to me. Then, "For the rest of your life when they see you coming down the street they'll say, 'Here come's the lady with only half a face because she tried to kill herself ha ha!'"

Up until now I had been thinking of my possible suicide as the result of human weakness. I was thinking people would feel sorry for me. But she saw it as the action of an idiot.

"Mom! Ha ha, hey mom! Listen! You might just take off your *nose*! Then you'll have to walk around for the rest of your life with a pair of those nose glasses on. You know, the ones they sell in Woolworths with the black mustaches!" She was rolling around the bed now, holding her stomach and laughing.

I asked myself, "Would *this* be her reaction if I did it?" What a way to go down in your kid's memory—"We won't talk about your dead grandmother, kids. She was an idiot!"

"Poor mom. A great big hole where your nose should be!"

"All right Sybil! That's enough!"

After she went to bed I found I couldn't light another cigarette. My hands refused to pick up the pack. For the first time in a decade I went to sleep without smoking my before-going-to-bed-cigarette.

The next morning I didn't smoke my before-I-get-out-of-bed-cigarette. Instead I got up, dressed and drove to town. At the wheel I talked to myself the way you talk to an alcoholic who needs to dry out. "If you ever needed help with anything, it's now. You've got to quit smoking! Wake up, you idiot! Don't ruin your life!"

Although it was only 8:00 a.m., the sun was already shining down on the courtyard around Caffe Pergolesi. After I parked my car I walked past the flower lady who was setting up her vases of gladiolus, irises, roses and gardenias and tulips. In the cafe I ordered a cappuccino. With my cup of coffee in hand I went outside again and sat down on a bench next to "The Wizard."

The Wizard is to the courtyard what the wooden Indian was to the cigar store. When he dies, most likely sitting there on that bench, they are going to bronze him in his familiar position of the yogi. Some credit the town's ambiance to his sitting there almost twenty-four hours a day. If this is true, then he is like the Pueblo Indians who take shifts watching the sun so that it will not fall down from the sky.

"How are you today?" he asked me as I sat down.

"Terrible," I told him. "I need to quit smoking and I don't want to."

"Yeah," he said, "it's all right to do those things when we're young, but as we get older our bodies need all the vital life energy they produce."

When he said the words "vital life energy" something snapped. Suddenly I didn't *have* to quit, I *wanted* to quit. I didn't want to burn up my body's energy with cigarette smoke.

"Our lungs and hearts work for us twenty-four hours a day and look how we treat them," he said. Zap. For the first time, my death wasn't in the future. It was right now. As long as I smoked I was living a less vital life than if I didn't smoke. I was only half alive. Was he a sorcerer? Was a curse lifted? How else was it possible that I would suddenly be so willing to do something I had spent years avoiding even until possible suicide?

Sitting there on that bench at 8:30 in the morning, I made the decision to quit smoking.

As I look back on it, I see that the magic had been wrought before I even sat down on the bench. The ground had been laid. The pump had been primed, not by a sorcerer but a sorceress: a seventeen year old joking girl who, the night before the morning, saved her mother's life.

7 Quitting

I was afraid I wouldn't be able to do it cold turkey and I didn't want an emotional kickback, so I made up a schedule. The first two weeks I smoked one cigarette every three hours: 9:00 a.m., 12:00 noon, 3:00, 6:00, 9:00. The second week I smoked only half a cigarette at those times. Every week after that I eliminated one of these hours.

The first night I ate half a bag of M&M's and a whole package of Pepperidge Farm's lemon cookies. I washed all this down with two Hanson Colas. The next day I was so depressed from all the sugar I'd eaten that I almost went back to smoking.

Every night after that I would turn on the TV and watch whatever came on the air: "Arnold," "Three's Company," "Dynasty," "The Colbys," cop shows, game shows. It really didn't matter what I watched as long as nobody was smoking on the program. I didn't want to have to think. I didn't want to do anything. I couldn't do anything. My brain was not able to absorb information. My brain had gone off to Hawaii, leaving my body to deal with this alone. The things people said to me went in one ear and out the other. My body was in shock. It was unsure of its borders, as in Woman Smashes Into Cement Reinforced Steel Divider On Freeway.

It was worse than any illness I've ever had. Worse than giving birth. Worse than a bad case of poison oak because you know the poison oak will go away soon. How did I know my craving would go away? I had friends who'd quit and kept their craving for ten years.

I had irrational mood swings. I said unpredictable things—such as the day I was sitting at Caffe Pergolesi when this guy on the other bench lit up a Camel.

"Excuse me," I said, "I used to smoke, too." Then I proceeded to tell him that he would feel much better about life if he quit smoking. I found myself telling him that I was going to start a therapy group for people who want to quit. My mouth was obviously taking revenge on me because I was not giving it a cigarette to puff on.

Hastily, before I said something I might never be able to live down, I went inside the Caffe and sat at a table. Only to find myself getting annoyed at the guy next to me who was rattling his newspaper. Irritated by the dishes clacking noisily behind the counter. Angry because people were talking too loud to one another. Paranoid, thinking the whole world was conspiring in chorus to stop me from quitting.

In a trance, my eyes dilated as wide as silver dollars. I walked the beaches, roamed the cafes and bookstores, haunted the library. I took out every book I could find on smoking—facts, history, the psychology of. I walked around town disoriented, embracing all the books in my arms, went at random into places I'd never been before—the pawn shop, the fish and tackle store. I found myself wandering aimlessly up and down the many-faceted aisles of Woolworths fingering plastic place mats, watching the parakeets under fluorescent lights, the goldfish swimming in their tank. I went into the material section. Kitchenware. Curtains. Children's toys.

I would have done just about anything to keep from going home. Home where it would be just me and the Throat Monster. Not until you quit smoking do you realize the Throat Monster lives inside you.

A sleeping dormant thing while I had remained true to my cigarette was now wide awake and, uncoiled, nagging me like a fisherman's wife.

"I want a cigarette."

"Boy, I sure could use a cigarette right now!"

"O.k.! Time for a cigarette!"

Once a friendly pal who was there to remind me when it would be nice to smoke a cigarette while reading, writing, talking, after eating or while drinking a cup of coffee, he was now torturing me. A one-time buddy who could now, at any moment, turn into a raving maniac screaming, "Give me a bloody cigarette or I'll make the rest of your life miserable!"

Being very intelligent, or should I say *exactly* as intelligent as I am, the Throat Monster knew just what to say to tempt me. It knew me as well as I knew myself and even used my own voice to speak to me with. If deduction didn't work, it used induction. If induction didn't work, it used threats, guilt, poetry, promises, philosophy, history, paranoia. Paranoia was its best device. It knew my weaknesses even better than I since its life depended on them. Here are some of the things the Throat Monster said to me:

"Tobacco is organic! It's a plant! God wouldn't have made it if he didn't want me to smoke it." The Throat Monster always used the personal pronoun "me" to fool the real me into thinking we were one and the same. This was just another gimmick, like:

"Indians smoked tobacco."

"I can have just one. What's that going to hurt?"

"The world is probably going to end soon anyway so what's the big deal? Go ahead . . . light one up!"

The torture wasn't just audio, it was visual. The moon, as it rose outside my window, would look like the burning tip of a cigarette. The stars as they came out one by one each looked like *smaller* burning tips of cigarettes. The Throat Monster would say, "It would be so nice to sit and look at the stars and smoke a cigarette right now." After I ate dinner I would want to smoke a cigarette. As I watched TV, as I read, my hands kept reaching for the pack.

Cigarettes! Cigarettes! Cigarettes! All the world's a cigarette and each cigarette plays its part. Everything that happened and some things that didn't happen became the Throat Monster's opportunity. Perhaps the phone would ring and it would be a wrong number. The Throat Monster would pounce saying, "Someone is harassing me! I need a cigarette!"

Or the phone *wouldn't* ring. Nobody called. This also became the Throat Monster's opportunity by turning it into a tragedy. He proceeded to list many other disappointments in my life and within the hour it would be that nobody had ever loved me or would ever love me, so what the hell? Why *not* smoke a cigarette?

Leaving the house in the morning wasn't that easy either. The Throat Monster went wherever I went. And as soon as I walked out my front door, the chances of slightly negative charged events were multiplied enormously. If a car pulled out of a side street sixty yards in front of me, it was trying to kill me. Every red light was a conspiracy of the City Council and the Road Department.

As a last avenue of escape I began reading the books I'd checked out of the library. It was then I came to know my demon in all his colors.

8 How Cigarettes and Cigarette Advertising Helped Shape World History

During the nineteenth century chewing was another way of taking tobacco. But by 1888 farmers, who left the rural life for higher-paying jobs in the city, learned that tobacco chewing and spitting were out in mixed company. It wasn't long before they learned to take their nicotine into their lungs, instead.

This we can credit to the efforts of one of the first ad men, Edward Featherstone Small. He employed the use of sex and power to get people to buy cigarettes by introducing the numbered card series with each pack. One card to a purchase, there were sets to be collected of actresses and men who had gone from rags to riches. These cards were the first bait used to get the "masses" to buy cigarettes.

Those who had already *gone* from rags to riches wouldn't have been caught dead smoking a cigarette. To give his cigarettes the Midas Touch, Buck Duke of American Tobacco hired Edward Small. If he could show the upper classes pictures of themselves smoking perhaps they would take up the habit along with caviar? Here we find the seed from which has sprouted modern advertising. Man has always learned to do things through imitation, the ad man simply has us imitate ourselves doing what he wants us to do.

By World War I cigarettes had reached the top rung of the social ladder and were associated with such patriotic ideals as dignity, bravery and endurance. Newspapers featured pictures of English, French, German and Russian soldiers at rest in the back lines smoking cigarettes. There were photos of the Kaiser lighting up and holding his pack out to a young grenadier. There was a news story that some Belgians sent an appeal to their minister of war. "Give us worse food if you like, but let us have tobacco."[1]

In the twenties the world began speeding up. During this time George Washington Hill, the President of American Tobacco, showed us that the image precedes the product. Hill took to advertising Lucky Strikes with the zeal of a fanatic. When he began his career in 1917 Americans were buying 30 billion cigarettes a year. "Before I die the total number of cigarettes sold in the U.S. annually will be from 200 billion to 225 billion," he bragged.[2] This very well may be the only modest statement the man ever made. When he died at sixty-one of a heart attack (most likely cigarette-related) over 300 billion a year were being sold.

George W. Hill looked like Marlon Brando's not as good looking younger brother. Hill was a short, pompous man who wore a big cowboy hat on his head, probably to make himself look taller. Instead of a gun in his hand, he carried a Lucky between his fingers. His limousine was crammed with packs of Luckies hanging down the windows on strings. It wasn't to protect the passengers that the car was manned by bodyguards, but to attract attention because he was a walking advertisement for his product.

Hill even grew tobacco plants in his flower beds at home.

Since he never missed a Lucky Strike commercial there was a radio in every room of his house. He'd turn up the sound whenever Lucky Strike commercials came on the air—forcing his guests to stop whatever they were doing, whether eating dinner or in the middle of a good conversation. There is a rumor that a reporter at a press conference once lit up a Camel in Hill's board room. Hill grabbed the foreign pack and threw it out the window. He then handed the reporter a carton of Luckies, instead.

Hill capsulized the method of his advertising genius once at a board meeting when he shocked his associates by spitting on the table. "That was a disgusting act," he said, "but none of you will ever forget it."[3]

And this was the manner in which the truth was spewed out. Hill understood that advertising is a weapon. He was awake enough to know that he was selling dreams and status, not *things*. Henceforth it was not the bar of soap you bought, but the cameo etched into it, not the durability of a car, but the cachet on the nameplate, not the actual tobacco, but the brand. It was the *idea* for which a brand had been named (Parliament, Viceroy, Kents, etc.) that seduced us into feeling dignified and respectable when we lit up.

Hill hired the best advertising man in the business, Edward Bernays, to aid him in his Lucky Strike crusade. Our first Dream Merchants, together they persuaded more people to smoke than any other individuals in history. They created an advertising idea around a product. They put the cart before the horse and it worked.

There were never two associates as different as these two. While Hill was impeccably dressed, Bernays was not always clean-shaven and resembled an absent-minded professor more than a businessman. While Hill was raw and loud, Bernays was so subtle you didn't know he was there. As a matter of fact, he wasn't there. Hill was reputed to have a precocious flair for hiring and firing ad men, but Bernays told him from the beginning that *he* did not work for Hill. If Hill wanted his services then he would have to come to Bernays's "Public Relations Council." Bernays's independent action gave advertising a professional identity separate from that of the manufacturer's product.

This is probably the reason Edward Bernays is known as the father of modern advertising. Fond of quoting the French writer Le Bons, Bernays had a penetrating understanding of the "whimsical monster," i.e., "the crowd." Bernays followed Le Bons's theories on crowd behavior, one of which is that "the crowd" is "less intelligent than the minds of the individuals that compose it."[4] Since "emotional states are contagious," Bernays mapped out America in an equation whose motion was dependent on public-relativity. Bernays's theory went something like this: $P = G.L. \times M.M.$ (Profit = Group Leader × Mass Mind). The direct route to the desires of the crowd was through its leaders. The best persuasive method is the one which never reveals itself.

Another born advertiser, P.T. Barnum, used this same method of subtlety. When he wanted Londoners to attend his circus, all P.T. Barnum did was issue an engraved invitation to the palace. The greatest "group leader" of them all, the Queen, then summoned both Barnum and Tom Thumb to St. James Palace. Barnum never once spoke directly to the audience he wanted to persuade but created events that the press and hence, the crowd, would follow.

Bernays took Barnum's unconscious ability for creating a circus around himself and made it into the conscious "new science" of public relations. It is fascinating that Bernays, the father of modern advertising, was the nephew of Sigmund Freud, the father of modern psychology. While Freud wanted to release the pent-up libido of the individual to free him (as much as possible) from neuroses, his American counterpart, Bernays, manipulated those same desires for a profit. It is said that Freud hated America and this may be the reason why.

The anniversary of the invention of the electric lightbulb

was only one of the opportunities Bernays seized upon for commercial interests. It was he who gathered Thomas Edison, Henry Ford and the President of the U.S. together in one room for the reenactment of that history-making moment in which the light bulb was discovered. Naturally the media tagged along behind these three great men and the electric light bill arrived in the mailbox not long after that.

In the twenties and thirties cigarette ads exalted technology and not only saluted the "modern" social changes, but sought to soothe any discomfort that might be caused by them. One of the things people found hard to reconcile themselves to was the loss of community feeling. Being just another fish in the ocean was the beginning of the Age of Anxiety—where the individual is pitted against the horde. It was to the ads people turned when they wanted to feel a part of things, whether this entailed wearing the correct garters or using the right soap. It was to the ads people unconsciously turned when they wanted to run away from the maddening crowd. Every time a Camel was lit the smoker could stare at the picture on the pack and go off on a fantasy adventure. But you would have not had to go to Egypt to find this particular camel. Barnum and Bailey owned the prototype dromedary pictured on the pack and had named him "Joe."[5]

All ad men knew about the good results generated by ads that were seen as a gesture of *intimacy*. Soon it was not only the product that loomed out of the crowd to become your friend. The creator of the product wanted to be your friend, too. The ads for Wilken Family Blended Whiskey were the best example of this kind of hokiness. After babbling on about Granny's cookies and Ma's hot mince pie, Pa Wilken told the audience how the Wilkens piled their boat up with the family whiskey before bringing it to market. "This photo shows you the Wilken Family giving a hand loading her up. It's me checking the number of cases with the captain, and my brother William wheeling a load up the gangplank. My brother-in-law Tom don't show up so good but you can make out the back part of him inside the barge bending over like."[6] The Wilkens ads went so far as to acquaint the audience with Jessie, the family dog. When Jessie gave birth to puppies, forty-five thousand people wrote the company asking for a photo.

By the 1930s Hill and his associates, Albert D. Lasker and Edward Bernays, had managed to make open smoking for middle class women popular. Before the age of advertising we know there were women who smoked, but this was usually done in a closet. On October 23, 1711, Jonathan Swift wrote of his wife Stella and her companion Mrs. Dingley, "Then there's the miscellany . . . an apron for Stella, a pound of chocolate, without sugar, for Stella, a fine snuff rasp of Ivory, given me by Mrs. St. John for Dingley, and a large roll of tobacco which she must hide or cut shorter out of modesty. . . ."[7]

The obituaries of 1845 have one Pheasy Molly fatally setting fire to her clothing at the age of ninety-six while lighting her pipe. In 1846 Charles Dickens found himself trapped in a room full of female smokers. "When I lighted my cigar, daughter lighted hers at mine: . . . Mother immediately lighted a cigar, American Lady immediately lighted hers: and in five minutes the room was a cloud of smoke. . . . Conceive this in a great hotel with not only their own servants but half a dozen waiters coming constantly in and out. I showed no atom of surprise, but I never was so surprised, . . . for in all my experience of ladies of one kind and another, I never saw . . . not a basket woman or a gypsy smoke before."[8]

The stepdaughter of the Quaker, Charles Fox, made entries in her accounts for tobacco and pipes bought for her mother and sister.

Early twentieth century advertisers left cigarettes out of the ads that had a woman in them. The actual pack of cigarettes was put at the bottom with the caption. Delicately women were wooed. It took time. We were courted. Then one day L&M ventured a little further. In 1926 Chesterfield advertisements pictured a couple sitting by a lake. The man was lighting a cigarette and the woman gazed up at him, in her eyes a look of respect and wonder. "Blow some my way," she coaxed. This was the indirect way to approach the female market.

The next year Philip Morris finally put women and cigarettes in bed together. In their ads women went all the way; we finally had the cigarettes in our mouths. They were smart enough to let us keep our purity at the same time by captioning the ad, "Women, When They Smoke At All, Quickly Develop Discriminating Taste." The inference? We choose our cigarettes the way we choose our men, with taste and discrimination. After all, we're not going to bed with just anybody.

Bernays, whose job it was to sell Luckies, wanted a theory to go along with the idea of a woman smoking. He hired a psychoanalyst, A.A. Brill, who then created the seed of the concept, "You've Come a Long Way Baby," with these words: "Some women regard cigarettes as symbols of freedom. More women now do the same work as men do. Many women bear no children, those who do bear have fewer children. Feminine traits are masked. Cigarettes, which are equated with man, become torches of freedom."[9]

Although women were finally smoking more, they still weren't smoking Luckies. Edward Bernays thought the color of the pack kept women away because green wasn't in vogue. But when he suggested they change the color of the pack, Hill didn't like it very much. "I've spent millions of dollars advertising the package. Now you ask me to change it. That's lousy advice."[10]

Instead of changing the package, Hill decided to try and change women. Where else would you approach a metamorphosis of this magnitude but through clothes? He decided he would make the new fashion color the same color as a pack of Lucky Strikes. Green. American Tobacco then paid for a strategic green fashion luncheon. Forums were sponsored where artists talked about how they used the color green in painting and psychologists talked about the beneficial effects of green on mental health. The coup de grace was a charity ball, given by a prominent socialite, at which women had to wear green gowns.

The ad men ambushed woman from all sides then lariated

her like they would a wild filly. They hired models and debu-
tantes to smoke Luckies in public after persuading them that
cigarette smoking was striking a blow for freedom and women.
Hill hired female European artists who gazed unabashed
straight out from the ads into the eyes of the crowd of American
women, sanctioning smoking for the female sex.

That year green did become the in fashion color. The ad
campaign had met with success! Except for one minor thing,
women still weren't smoking Luckies. Women were playing
hard to get with Hill. The more they didn't want to smoke his
cigarettes the more feverishly he seemed to pursue them.

When Amelia Earhart flew over the Atlantic, Lucky
Strikes came out with ads showing her in her flight regalia with
the caption, "Lucky Strikes were the cigarettes carried on the
'Friendship' when Amelia Earhart crossed the Atlantic." Although it was at this time more women began to smoke publicly,
one foot was kept on the pedestal. Many women did not want to
associate themselves with Earhart's masculine image and did
not take up smoking Luckies. Actually, we never did take up
smoking them. Most of us stayed away from Luckies the way we
stay away from pool halls, cock fights and card games. We aren't
as stupid as Hill would have liked to believe. We have our
intuition. We know that Amelia may have gone down for a
cigarette. We know that it might have been the craving for a
Lucky Strike that got her lost out there in the wild blue yonder.
What if she dropped her pack of Luckies out the window and
went overboard reaching for them? What if she blew up the
plane while she was lighting one up?

Hill must have worked himself into a dither as he waited
impatiently for women to fall in love with his so far unrequited
Lucky Strikes. He even tried to reach women's hearts through
boxes of bonbons—but not by leaving them on their doorsteps,
by taking them away. Early in the Depression while some people
were jumping out of twelve-story windows and most were eating
beans, Hill attacked candy, the most frivolous food—a minus
nutrient.

Hill didn't just *ignore* the Depression, he seemed to take a perverse enjoyment in satirizing it. One envisions hungry men, women and children walking down the street. A winter wind bites into their lean bones as they trudge along with their heads down so as not to miss a peanut, potato or a piece of bread on the ground that may have fallen out of someone's basket. They turn the corner and are confronted suddenly by a billboard the size of the Goodyear blimp. On it the actress, Constance Talmadge, is smiling down at them saying, "Light a Lucky and you'll never miss sweets that make you fat." Was this a mirage? An oasis in the desert? They even got Helen Hayes to do a testimonial saying that the use of Luckies instead of sweets accounted for the trim figure of the modern female.

"A good advertising fight helps both sides," Hill had said. By this time Schraffts had retaliated by removing Lucky Strikes from their counters. Next they bombed the cigarette companies with bonbon advertisements such as "Do not let anyone tell you a cigarette can take the place of a piece of candy. The cigarette will inflame your tonsils, poison with nicotine every organ of your body, and dry up your blood-nails in your coffin."

Candy ads now came out with new amazing discoveries as to the value of candy. Suddenly candy became the mainstay of a "scientific reducing regime." One ad, put out by the National Confectioners' Association, had a photo of a plate of bonbons under the heading "You can get thin comfortably on candy." The ad read like an article straight out of *Scientific American*:

How to Reduce Comfortably on Candy

The main trouble with most reducing diets is that they make the subject uncomfortable, lower resistance, and produce weakness.

In the Gorden-von Stanley regime this does not happen. You simply eat moderately restricted meals, with candy between meals!

The candy between meals is eaten during exercise, whenever you are hungry, tired or nervous, to the amount of about one third of a pound a day for an adult.[11]

Many people were irritated at the cigarette industry for publicly attacking candy, which was another product altogether and not in competition with Lucky Strikes. In defense of the candy war, Hill wrote an essay titled: "The Newer Competition," published in *World's Work*, in 1929. This piece ought to be studied more for its propaganda style than its content. In it he not only justified his campaign against candy but made it seem like a necessary cause. The purpose of the new competition was to create more products of various kinds for the "crowd" to buy. As usual, war was good for the marketplace.

Personally, I don't believe Hill wrote this article. Hill could never have gone the distance in this somber essay form; he would have clicked his heels midway and jumped the fence. But what a typical ad move this would have been for the man behind Hill—the man who *wasn't there*, Bernays.

Thanks to the candy war the plump look was now out for women. And the candy ads began to read like a call for help from a people losing the battle. "Don't neglect your candy ration!" "Read how candy saves wear and tear on body tissues—how candy can help you to your proper weight!" As late as 1948 the National Confectioners Association's Council on Candy was running ads like the one in the Saturday Evening Post that started out saying, "Wouldn't you like some candy?"

Which is more dangerous, candy or cigarettes? It is an intriguing question. The reality is that when one smokes, the body is depleted of energy so that in order to maintain a balance, it craves a sugar fix. Candy and cigarettes ought to have worked together as a team. They would have complemented each other. Hill and Schrafft's should have created a campaign with the slogan, "You can have your cigarettes and eat your cake!" Better yet, Hill could have sold Schrafft's the rights to the packaging and labeling for candy Lucky Strikes. They could have ignored all the other issues and gone for a combination of the two: "Eat a Chocolate *and* Light a Lucky at the Same Time!"

Even though thin was now in, women still wouldn't touch a Lucky. One envisions Hill in his limo riding down the populated streets of New York City looking askance at the women. Disillusioned, he asks his bodyguards indignantly, "What do they want? What do they have against me? What did I ever do to them?"

During the Depression, Americans gave up food but not cigarettes. Still, afraid of losing customers, the cigarette companies competed with each other through advertising instead of lowering their prices.

Hill carried this to comical extremes. Instead of taking the role of a philanthropist, he took the role of Dr. Strangelove. The first thing he did was give his cigarettes intrigue by commenting that only three people in the world possessed the secret formula for Lucky Strike. Assuming he was one of the three, his refusal to name the others added further mystery to the situation. Could it be that the formula holders would be in danger if their identities were known? Would thugs kidnap and torture them into giving out the recipe? Would a Mata Hari-type vamp offer her body for the information? At least now his two bodyguards had character parts.

Reynolds agents spread rumors that dangerous chemicals were used in the Lucky Strike formulae. Hill's ad men retaliated by suggesting that sheep dip was used when growing all tobacco and only Lucky Strike removed it with the toasting process.[12]

The demand for cigarettes continued high in 1930. Now that the country's smokers were hooked, the companies reeled them in. But *not* by lowering their prices. Reynolds went from two packs for a quarter to fifteen cents a pack. Seemingly the reason was because they changed the glassine wrapper to a humidor pack. But this was a facade done to pacify the consumer.

To compensate, there was a move back to roll-your-owns. In 1931 a nickel bag of Bill Durham could supply one with twenty cigarettes. Bull Durham's sales went from 22,000 to

60,000 pounds a day. But when several people tried to market simple rolling machines the cigarette companies had the Commissioner of Internal Revenue, David Burnet, check through the lawbooks. There he found Article 62, Regulation 8, which forbids not only demonstrating and selling rollers in tobacco stores but rolling-your-own on the premises.[13]

The tobacco companies never recognized the existence of the "loosie" trade because it would have ruined the upbeat image they wanted to project. While people stood freezing in bread lines, huddled together under blankets to keep warm, the cigarette companies sponsored radio programs featuring comedy and swing bands. Between the years 1930–32 George W. Hill's income was at an all-time high of $2,800,000.[14]

In 1940 prosperity was on the rise while, at the same time, the country was worried about war. This combination helped boost the sales of cigarettes after the Depression. Impulse smoking, often not possible during the hard times, started up again. Furthermore, smoking was hyped up as an acceptable way to reduce tension; the more perilous the situation, the more appropriate a cigarette. It was no accident that soldiers smoked more than civilians. By the early 1940s ads were barraging us with pictures of soldiers and sailors smoking.

Army officers ranked cigarettes among the big three on their list of morale necessities, after mail and food. During World War II Douglas MacArthur congratulated civilian workers in the defense industry for raising hundreds of thousands of dollars toward the War effort. He suggested, "The entire amount should be used to buy American cigarettes which of all the personal comforts are the most difficult to obtain here."[15] After President Roosevelt declared tobacco an essential crop, draft deferments were given to tobacco growers.

Suddenly the ads became super patriotic. They now featured soldiers, sailors and pilots. One Camels ad during the war had a picture of a flyer with a cigarette between his lips, saying, "You Want Steady Nerves When You're Flying Uncle Sam's

Bombers Across the Ocean." At the bottom of the ad was this hilarious caption: "Names withheld for defense purposes and national security."

During the war Lucky Strikes and Chesterfield encouraged radio show bandleaders to do Bob Hope-type goodwill stints. A special offer on paydays gave draftees a chance to buy three cartons of Camels for the price of one. A pack a day would cost each soldier $4.50 a month, which is a large chunk out of the twenty-one dollar a month paycheck they earned in the service. Probably as much as a cocaine habit would be today for someone who earned $2,000 a month.

Of course the most conniving of them all was Hill, who took ADvantage of the wartime situation to finally change the unlucky color of the Lucky Strike package. Until now he hadn't found a graceful way of altering it so that women might be more attracted to the wrapper.

In 1942, the green pack was replaced by a white one of the same basic design with a new slogan, "Lucky Strike Green Has Gone to War!" American Tobacco hoped the public would believe that it had discontinued use of the green color in order to free the ink for the war effort. For what? Camouflage paint? Lucky Strike green was not needed by any branch of the defense effort.

Meanwhile soldiers received a pack of smokes in their field rations along with dehydrated soup, lemonade mix and their can of Spam. It should come as no surprise that by disarmament day, the average GI was smoking fifty-eight cigarettes a day.

Shortly after, a quasi-barter system developed in Europe because the currency was untrustworthy. A new currency was needed. One that was easy to carry, hard to counterfeit and possessed an intrinsic value—like cigarettes. In Austria in 1946 a carton was worth $100. Vienna apartments were rented for two packs a month. By 1945 Luckies, Camels and Chesterfields became the money supply in Germany.

Several smokes could buy a fine piece of Dresden china

and a couple of cartons would get an excellent camera. Half of a pack of cigarettes paid for a hearty dinner and, afterwards, an evening with a prostitute. Waiters and taxi drivers accepted a two-cigarette tip. You could buy anything you wanted with cigarettes, from shoes to fake papers. Cigarettes even affected the criminal justice system. In 1947 Hamburg police offered a one thousand American cigarette reward for information pertaining to a local murder.

One Italian selling cigarettes on the black market in France was unable, when picked up by the police, to speak any French or English except the three magic words which had earned him $500 a week for the six months previous, "Chesterfields, Luckies and Camels."[16]

In Germany cigarettes were worth $140 a carton. Americans rented and furnished their apartments with cigarettes. German workers preferred to be paid in cigarettes rather than unstable marks. Naturally, nobody smoked cigarettes. Instead they smoked butts that cost between three cents and seven cents, depending on the length.

The height of cigarette power was reached when a legal barter center opened in Berlin in August, 1946.[17] American soldiers marched through one door carrying their cartons of cigarettes while German civilians filed through the other door lugging all the possessions they wanted to trade for cigarettes: silver, art, china, cameras, radios and furs. In the early 1940s Hermann Goering had pillaged Europe's galleries. Now the Americans were doing the same thing in Berlin, but in a completely American way. G.I.s mailed art objects to their relatives, who sold them for a killing. Until Europe became flooded with smokes, that is, and cigarette inflation set in. At this point, the owner of packs of cigarettes smoked their shares to cut down on the supply.

9 Sometimes You've Got to Get Sick to Get Well

*T*he following was recorded on cassette three weeks after I had initiated the quitting process. The voice is hoarse, not to mention weak, as if the person speaking was dying:

(Cough cough) The flu has struck me down. I can't leave the house. Now there's nothing to keep me from thinking about *them*. My body aches, my head is throbbing, I have no energy, I can hardly lift myself out of bed (cough cough) in order to go to the bathroom. I lie here like, ha, a dead person (cough). Oh the irony! I wonder, can the Throat Monster create (cough cough) physical illness to get me to smoke again? We live in a cynical universe. My temperature is 100 degrees today. I can't lift the knitting needles and my quitting smoking scarf sits on the ledge of the loft still only four inches long (cough cough). It's all I can do to push the start button on this recorder. I can't even smoke the few meager puffs left on my schedule.

What started out as a headache progressed to nasal congestion, diarrhea, stomach ache, then a fever. Thinking I had arthritis, I went to the doctor (cough) and she told me I have the flu. I am quarantined. No one will visit me. My only company is TV. I turn it on every morning at 8:00 a.m. and watch "Good Morning America." At 9:00 I watch "Phil Donahue" (cough cough). I talk to myself on my tape recorder.

I'm not only sick physically but I'm sick emotionally. I've been lying up here in bed mourning the loss of my cigarette and my grief would not be much different if I had lost a friend (cough) or lover. Of course, it was not love at first sight. When I first met Mr. Cigarette I was repulsed by him. It took time for him to grow on me before I *really* wanted him. Needed him. Couldn't live without him.

We made a great couple. No matter how bad I was feeling my cigarette was always there to comfort me (cough cough). We not only looked good together but got along well at parties. I was secure with him. Even though he knew me inside and out my cigarette loved me just as I was. Every puff (cough) was a satisfying kiss between my lips and my cigarette. Life was idyllic.

When I was down he was there to console me. When I was up he was there to celebrate along with me. When I drank he was always in the hand that held the glass. Every party invitation, it was understood, was for me and my cigarette. Reservations at a restaurant? For two. A vacation in Hawaii? For me and you-know-who.

When I got married no lover was ever more understanding of my growing needs, less jealous, more compliable, reliable and available. Why? Because my cigarette knew that as the years went by I would easily be able to spend a day away from my husband, but never *him*. While in human relationships intimacy often breeds contempt this was never so between me and my cigarette. Au contraire. The more time we spent together (cough) the more firmly we were wedded—until death might have us parted. As it turned out I eventually left my husband and my cigarettes went out the front door with me.

•   •   •

Fever at 101. I haven't been sick for five years, why *now*? Unless . . . (cough) . . . this is related to quitting cigarettes.

Unless my body has (cough) gotten a signal to detoxify and this germ that's going around was welcomed to hasten my cleaning out. What a good body you are. How faithful! (cough cough).

◆   ◆   ◆

I've been flat on my back for a week now. I'm so sick I don't even (cough) want a cigarette. It's my brain that wants one. My brain wants to keep the craving alive. It's grown used to wanting a cigarette and having the wish answered. My brain is (cough cough) bored, I think.

◆   ◆   ◆

It's been raining for thirteen days straight as if the whole world was cleaning itself with me. My sister (cough) came by this morning to bring me some food. I thought she'd (cough) just hand me the grocery bag through the window. But instead she actually walked into my germ-infested house and set the bag down on the table in the living room below my loft. She stood there and withdrew a bottle of 7 Up and Squirt.

"Do you want me to get sicker or better?" I asked her because these are the kinds of things our mother used to give us when we were ill back in the fifties.

"Michael—the guy who owned Michael and Company— that beauty salon? He just died from the flu," she said. (cough cough)

She was making me feel better by the minute. "Are you kidding? That's terrible! How did he die?"

"His lungs got infected. He caught pneumonia. He was only thirty-three years old."

"Poor guy."

"Yeah. You'd better take care of yourself." As soon as she said this, she started backing away toward the door. (cough)

I was hanging down over the edge of my loft, hungry for companionship. The only non-TV person I'd seen in two weeks was leaving. I groped for something to say to keep her there. "Well, I'm sure I'll get a lot better with this stuff you brought me. How's Stefan?" (her son.)

She was halfway (cough) out the door that leads to my back porch. "He's fine. And he's going to stay fine." Now she was standing in the rain on my back porch.

"And how's Eric?" (her husband.)

"He's fine, too."

"How's (cough) Rosie?" (her dog.)

"Fine."

"How's . . . well, how are *you*?"

"I'm fine, but I won't be if I don't get away from you."

I had a coughing fit here and she left, saying, "I'll call you later."

Now I was alone again except for the bottles of Squirt and 7 Up she'd brought me, as a family joke. I thought about my childhood. Life sure was strange in the fifties. People didn't think they had to eat real food. Back then people really believed Wonder Bread helped build their bodies—what was it . . . twelve ways? As far as my mother was concerned all we had to do was eat food that had the right name and we would not only survive, we would thrive. Our orange juice wasn't squeezed from real oranges but fizzed its way to us from the "magic crystals" in a jar. Pulp and peel were irrelevant beside the word Tang! on the label. Here in a seventy-nine cent jar my mother had captured all the zip, zest and razzmatazz of life. Cheerios had nothing to offer nutrition either but it was such an uplifting name to have before us on the table at the beginning of each new day. We would probably have relished dog food if it had come to us labeled "Super Human Stew."

10 When My Kingdom Comes I'll Have a Hamburger, a Coke and a Cigarette

LADY BRACKNELL:. . . Do you smoke?
ERNEST: Well, yes, I must admit I smoke.
LADY BRACKNELL: I am glad to hear it. A man should always have an occupation of some kind.

OSCAR WILDE
The Importance of Being Earnest

*I*f aliens came to planet Earth in the 1950s, they would have thought cigarettes were the way we maneuvered ourselves about. If they'd wanted us to become their slaves all they would have had to do was take our cigarettes away from us and then dole them out for good behavior. Surely they would have thought we were not air breathers but smoke inhalers who could only exist on this oxygen-filled planet by carrying around white cylinders filled with smoke.

Adults in the fifties had been raised on cigarette advertisements which invited themselves to family holidays. In the ads cigarettes were guests present while trimming the tree and carving the turkey. Adults in the fifties had grown up watching "Santa Claus racing his convertible at excessive speeds on behalf of high octane gasoline, smoking a Lucky Strike, stealing a kiss 'from a ravishing Old Gold maiden'" or gulping down "a straight slug of Old Drum blended whiskey."[1] No wonder Bette Davis snatched a cigarette as soon as she discovered she was ill in that movie. She'd been weaned on ads like the Luckies one which read, "When all else fails I'm your best friend." Cigarettes were no longer inanimate objects. The ads brought them to life so they could be our companions. And a Lucky was "a better friend than others, in personal tragedies, minor or major" because "a Lucky stands you in good stead."[2] Underneath the plain white wrappings lurked the hearts of Florence Nightingales, psychiatrists and social workers. It's no wonder then that in 1958, when R.J. Reynolds wanted to move the Pyramid on the Camel pack from the right side of the picture back into the distance, the company received several truckloads of angry letters.

In the fifties cigarettes were easier to find than a drink of water. As a matter of fact, they were a part of our diets, along with hamburgers, french fries, and Coke. Now, instead of single packs, cartons were purchased. There were one- and two-carton families. The average smoker consumed one-and-one-half packs a day.

In the fifties cigarette packs stuck out of men's suit pockets along with handkerchiefs and credit cards. They were on the dashboards of cars, in the glove compartments, on the desk at the office. Baseball, football, and track stars' endorsements were used in advertising as if cigarettes helped fuel athletic ability. Marie Antoinette had it all wrong when she said, "Let them eat cake!" It was cigarettes we wanted.

Do not fire until you see the whites of their cigarettes!

Give me a cigarette or give me death!

Perhaps this was the fault of advertisements such as the one for Camels in *American Magazine*, 1926. The picture was of a small town Fourth of July parade and the caption read, "When Fourth of July bands are playing and the cannons are roaring out their celebration of another day of Independence and Freedom—have a Camel!" It wasn't enough for Camel to associate itself with just *one* day, however. This ad went on to link cigarettes up with the broader concept of freedom itself, "For no other cigarette ever brought such liberation to so many millions of smokers."[3]

In the fifties cigarettes had already become a part of the American male's puberty ceremony. Teenage boys had them rolled up in the sleeves of their T-shirts and sticking out from behind their ears—protruding like adolescent chest hairs.

For many women of the fifties life became a twenty-four-hour-a-day cigarette break thanks to canned food, Hamburger Helper and washing machines. Originally it was the appeal by advertisers to upper class sophistication that wooed and won women over to smoking. They told us that the feminine archetype could smoke. In the early ads women were allowed to remain on the pedestal and smoke at the same time.

Women in the fifties kicked the pedestal out from under their feet like an orange crate. While grocery shopping they wore their hair in curlers and had cigarettes sticking out of their mouths. They carried their cigarettes in their purses or clutched the packs in their hands along with lighters.

In the fifties it was not unusual to go in for a medical checkup and have your doctor smoking while the two of you discussed your lung x-ray. Not uncommon to have him *offer* you one from his pack in the breast pocket of the white jacket behind the stethoscope, as you sat on the table. "Well, Bob, there's a pretty big dark spot right here. . . . Say, would you like a smoke? . . . . I just don't know what the problem is. It looks like we may have to operate. . . . Oh, here, let me light it for you. . . . Let's see, you do have Blue Cross, don't you, Bob?"

Mysteriously, it became impossible for anyone to drive anywhere without smoking a cigarette at the wheel.

More school children in the 1950s memorized the lines

Winston Tastes Good
Like A Cigarette Should

than had ever learned a Shakespearean sonnet. Leave it to the advertisers to learn how to make money from poetry when even the poets can't. This little rhyme took Reynolds Tobacco Co. up from $7.5 billion earnings in 1954 to $23 billion in 1955.[4] If the purpose, role of the artist, is to express the collective unconscious in order to provide catharsis, as in the Greek dramas, then how much have these often-repeated slogans affected our dreams and aspirations, which in turn shape our outer reality?

In the fifties cigarette companies continued to claim that smoking aided digestion. Reynolds boasted that more doctors smoked Camels than any other cigarette. "Julips" (whatever *they* were) aided in clearing up head colds. Kools went even further, proclaiming itself as a *preventative* for colds. Many New York doctors recommended king-size cigarettes to their patients. The rationalization was that king-size smokes acted as a natural filter.

For the cigarette companies the only question was how to lure us into smoking more than the amount we were already smoking. One gets the feeling that if they had it their way we would be smoking two or three cigarettes at once.

They had already succeeded in getting us smoking more than one at a time by changing the length. They did this simply by taking already popular brands and stretching them into Cadillacs. Women tended to smoke the king-size more than men—perhaps because they could burn in an ashtray longer while doing the dishes. Or was it because the new streamlined length emphasized long, shapely fingernails?

Even as a fresh army of statistics was marching over the horizon, ad men sat huddled around boardroom tables thinking of ways to sell more cigarettes.

11 Movies: The Survival of the Glamourest

Movies packed cigarettes with the selling power of a rocket fueled for Jupiter. The movie screen was a bigger than life Medusa tempting us to smoke through glorifying cigarettes along with the actors. Tobacco lobbyists were constantly at work in Hollywood trying to get movie stars to smoke in their films. In his book *Hollywood*, Garson Kanin tells how he was offered a "handsome gift" if he could implore Ginger Rodgers to puff on a cigar in one of her movies that he was directing. Why? The movie screen is a reflecting pool for our idealized versions of ourselves. I remember the effect Bette Davis had on me as a teenager smoking my first cigarette. Somehow she would not have been the gutsy dame she was without puffing on all those cigarettes.

We are as gullible as monkeys when we're at the movies. The film version of any person, place or thing mesmerizes us. It is as if film affects a part of our brain we have not yet met. What we are seeing on the screen is somehow unexplainable to us, therefore unaccountable, therefore all the more powerful in its sway over us. Always for mankind it has been the unapproach-

able that has held the most power. The images become un-
spoken supernaturals and register as godlike in our minds. All
the more valued for their fragility and vulnerability to over-
exposure. All the more exalted for their fading and evaporating
right before our eyes. All the more immortal for their temporary
(two hour) existence.

Just as the Greeks projected their gods as the shapers of
material reality, we use our movie projectors to put our stars
before us as the movers of life. Gradually the movie star has
evolved into The Unreachable Star that will somehow guide us,
protect us the way the gods and goddesses used to. Why do they
have this power? Because they are bigger than us, approximately three times our size. They are brighter than us, spot-
lighted as if by the sun itself.

The influence of movies upon manners and morals is far-
reaching. When Clark Gable wore no undershirt in *It Happened
One Night*, it hurt the undershirt industry. Rudolph Valentino's
shiny hair affected a generation of men and boys. After his
movies came out, thousands of men doused their heads with
Brilliantine. The fashion industry has done well by movies.
Actresses wear a different dress in every scene, even if they play
characters who work in a drug store. Women come to the theatre
to see what the stars are wearing as much as the movie. And they
(scratch that, we) still do. *Annie Hall* set baggy pants and jacket
fashion for a decade to follow. Meryl Streep as Isak Dinesen in
Out of Africa really got khaki going. No wonder the tobacco
companies wanted to get their cigarette protegees into the
movies.

Cigarettes were a sign of effeminacy in Europe during
most of the nineteenth century. It was the theatres, then the
movies, that eventually legitimized them for the "man's man."
In early films, cigarettes were seen as "dainty" things. In Cecil
B. DeMille's *The Plainsman* Wild Bill Hickok (played by Gary
Cooper) sees his first cigarette while on a Mississippi paddle
steamer. "Hey, mister," he says to the passenger who is smoking

it, "Your toothpick is on fire!" To which the other man replies, "That's no toothpick, that's a *cigareet*. It's the latest fashion way down East."[1]

Early in the Depression several companies, led by Warner Brothers, released films of social conscience in which the criminal, a member of the lower class, portrayed by such actors as Cagney, Bogart and George Raft, smoked cigarettes. Even while gunning down their enemies. In a movie called the *Petrified Forest*, Humphrey Bogart was the first rough type to smoke. After he portrayed Detective Sam Spade, who was lighting up a Lucky Strike in just about every scene in the *Maltese Falcon*, the image of the tough guy who smokes was etched into the public mind. In *The Treasure of the Sierra Madre*, Bogart is murdered out in the middle of nowhere for want of a cigarette.

> MEXICAN BANDIT: "Have you got a cigarette?"
> BOGART: "No, I haven't. But I've got a few pinches of tobacco if that will do."
> MEXICAN BANDIT: "Any paper to roll it in?"
> BOGART: "I've got a bit of newspaper."[2]

Not good enough. The bandit (who probably wanted a Lucky Strike) kills Bogie with his own machete.

These men were looked upon as heroes. They also played the roles of FBI agents and policemen. In the same movies, their wives and girlfriends—Ann Sheridan, Bette Davis, Joan Crawford, Lana Turner, Lauren Bacall and Jane Russell—also smoked. In the movie *Caged*, Eleanor Parker plays a woman who goes from innocence to corruption when she's put in a women's prison. She is rolling-her-own when she leaves. In *The Company She Keeps*, Jane Greer makes her own with a rolling machine. "Something wrong with rolling my own?" she asks her parole officer. "It's a prison habit. I wouldn't do it if I were you," the parole officer replies. Greer begins buying packs in a drugstore. In *Remember My Name* Geraldine Chaplin pinched her butts out with two fingers.[3]

Almost all the films of the forties and fifties seem to be

saying that to be a hero or heroine you must first be addicted to cigarettes. To be able to catch a crook or fall in love or get rich, to have charisma and adventure in your life, you must smoke. Nothing of any consequence happened in the movies without somebody lighting a cigarette first so that the cylinders of tobacco seemed to be event makers. The invisible man became visible when he lit his cigars.

Movies were the best advertising cigarettes ever had. They not only put the poetry of the ads in motion, but brought them giant size before our eyes. Movies were every cigarette company's dream come true just as they were ours. They inferred the reality the way magazines never could and cost nothing to the manufacturer except, perhaps, for bribe money.

12 The Victim

*T*he following was recorded after eleven days in bed (Fever and cough gone, along with urge for cigarette):

Today Phil Donahue interviewed a woman smoker who wants to form a coalition of all smokers. She feels the government is taking away their freedom by banning smoking in public places. She said the First Amendment guarantees her the right to smoke wherever and whenever she wants to.

"I enjoy smoking," she said. "I don't want to quit! Banning smoking from public places is a violation of individual freedom!"

Audience consensus: Her smoke invades the space of others. When an individual uses his or her freedom to poison others, they are using it as a weapon.

"I'm sick and tired of the government trying to control our lives," she said. I think she expected to get some supporters with this statement because she paused the way they do on TV when they think the audience is going to clap. She refused to believe it when a member of the audience pointed out that she enjoys smoking merely because she is addicted to nicotine.

Addicts will go to any length lying to themselves and others in order to feed their addiction. Although her personality seemed like the opposite of a victim's, the one who refuses to be victimized by an outside force, she is actually the queen of victims. She won't allow anyone to intervene in her hurting herself. "Nobody can hurt me but me. You will hurt me if you don't let me hurt me."

All smokers are victims. Every time I felt insulted, hurt, cornered, paranoid, I would smoke a cigarette. It's just like saying, "Go ahead! I deserved that! No, I deserve *more* than that! I'll finish the job for you by smoking a cigarette." Of course, I also smoked when I felt happy.

To be a good victim you have to be greedy. You have to feel that you are the center of the universe. You have to see the whole of life as out to get you. *You* have to be *that* important. Everyone else must come into existence in order to torture you. *You* are what life is all about.

One gets the feeling that if the victim was suddenly lifted off the Earth and carried away on a magic carpet to another world, a more beneficent world than ours where Mr. Kindness and Mrs. Generosity reigned, they would ask for a ticket back home again. This is because being saved brings death to the victim.

Being saved is not what victims want. They want to *need* to be saved. The perfect balance for the smoker who wants to be a hardcore victim would be to quit smoking for two days and then go back to smoking for two days. Quit for two more days, go back, quit, go back.

◆   ◆   ◆

Upon leaving college I became a caretaker so that I could live in nature and not be victimized by the stressful artificial environment of a city. What a great example I would have been if I hadn't been a chain-smoker.

My first caretaking job was in a vineyard located on the gently sloping foothills around San Jose. Here I had my own house right in the middle of the grapes. This house had been built by the original wine maker many years before. He smoked, too. By the time I moved into the house he was dying of emphysema. Every Saturday morning he drove up at 9:00 a.m. sharp to water the rose garden he'd planted by the side of the house thirty years ago. This was his life's last pleasure. He could barely make it from the car to the rose bushes. He could barely talk. As he explained to me how he used to make champagne by adding one of these rosebuds to the bottle his words were interrupted by short gasps. One day he didn't come anymore. I was too young and immortal to think that smoking could ever do the same to me.

I remember sitting on the front steps of this old rickety house and how the grapes all around me shone like rows of emeralds at twilight while I smoked cigarettes. When I think back on my life—the adventures, all the ideal places—no matter where or what, I always had a cigarette between my fingers.

When I lived on a farm in Watsonville I smoked a pack a day. First thing in the morning before collecting the chickens' eggs, last thing at night before going to sleep. There I had a small cottage set in the middle of a cow pasture. I even had my own horse. There is a photo of me on that horse, smoking a cigarette.

I've spent most of my life chain-smoking my way through the countryside. I remember caretaking on top of a mountain in Bonny Doon so high it almost touched heaven. There I had almost everything heaven could offer: my own cabin, a swimming pool. The people I worked for were gone to Europe half the year and I had a lot of time to sit and enjoy the heavenly view of the ocean ten miles below. I produced some terrific metaphysical thoughts here while smoking my cigarettes.

After cigarette smoking and writing (frankly I'm not sure which is #1) gardening has been my third greatest passion in life. I remember living on another farm, this one a Christmas tree farm, and working in my vegetable garden. Every hour on the hour I would smoke a cigarette. The pack and the matches were always waiting on top of the fence post. I would work all day long not stopping once except to smoke. There must be a thousand cigarette butts mashed down in the soil of that garden. The people who live there now must think I was using cigarettes for fertilizer.

13 *If You Can Think It, It's REAL*

The biggest misconception in psychology is that neurosis is an abnormal state. We're all closet neurotics. Neurosis is normal! The reason for this is we all think. Thoughts are like rabbits you pull out of a hat. They multiply themselves. They divide. They grow BIG. And then they shrink and get so small we can hardly see them anymore until they go away altogether—suddenly to reappear in a place they aren't supposed to be like a bull in a China shop. Thoughts are hard to manage and, after all, we are only human. It would be nice if they were like trees, rivers, fauna and flora—things that do not shift constantly like the trickster's pea under the walnut. It would be a lot easier if our thoughts could be rooted in the ground. Tomorrow when we wake up, our maple tree will not be on the other side of the world. But we have no idea what direction our thinking is going to take.

It is very difficult to be held responsible for everything our thinking has created. There is so much of it, visible and invisible. One of the things that our thinking has created is smoking.

It is a myth that a person needs to smoke to be happy. We did not come into this world needing to smoke to be happy.

There were no cigarettes scotch-taped to our little butts upon arrival. And if it is true that we linger on after we die—if we have reservations waiting for us in heaven, or some other dimension, or some other planet—there is not going to be a pack of our favorite brand of cigarettes waiting for us on our bedstand there. You can be sure that if there is such a thing as eternal life, we are going to go through *all* of it not smoking a single cigarette.

We all know people who have been heavy smokers and then quit. Usually when you ask them how they managed to accomplish this they shrug their shoulders and say they just woke up one morning, decided not to smoke anymore, and then never thought about it again.

Not thinking about it is the secret. For those of us stuck in the smoking rut this is infuriating. That's because mentally we are obsessed with the *idea* of smoking. The difficulty in quitting is not so much the body's addiction to the nicotine as the thinker's addiction to the idea of nicotine. It is the habit of thinking we need cigarettes, not the cigarettes themselves, that keeps us prisoners of our habit. In Sartre's play *No Exit*, the characters couldn't find their way out of a self-created hell composed of their thoughts. If we want to stop smoking, we have to learn how to not think about smoking!

The craving for a cigarette is a program we created. It runs on automatic. We made it, we can destroy it. In order to defeat the cigarette program the body is running on it helps to know how the interdependency of our body and brain works automatically. When we smoke cigarettes we are in a deceitful relationship with our bodies because we are lying to them about life. We are telling our bodies that poison should make them happy. The craving for a cigarette is an artificial dependency. It is not the natural state for a body to be in. It is just that we grow so used to this artificial level of functioning, the body either stops sending the brain signals that something is wrong, or our brain stops processing these signals. This is known as autonomic conditioning, i.e., to become comfortable with an uncomfortable state.

Mosquitos do it and so do flies when they adapt to man-made repellents.

Our hearts normally beat seventy-three times per minute. When we smoke one cigarette the heartbeat goes up to somewhere around ninety-five. When we "feel" that we are "in the mood" for another cigarette—such as while having a cup of coffee (the cigarette's sidekick) or when someone else is lighting up, what is *really* happening is that our hearts have gradually been returning to their normal baseline rate of seventy-three beats per minute. It is at this time we experience "craving" (discomfort). If we were a car, this would be the moment we ran out of gas. Time for a fill up! Except our brain and body are saying, "Help! I need a cigarette." What they are really saying is, "I need to get back to my artificial level of functioning! I need to get back to my induced environment again! Help! This is what I'm used to!" Since it takes one hour for the heart to return to the normal seventy-three beats per minute, we want a cigarette every hour on the hour so we can stay in the speed lane. Our hearts are tired and in a constant state of overexertion.

Give a baby a cigarette and it will go into convulsions. Pay no heed to the messages of stress sent to the brain by the body when in need of help and it stops sending the conscious part of our minds any message at all. It is at this point the robot smoker has taken over.

Our brains react to our bodies. For a heavy smoker, the world is viewed through a screen of poison and stress. When we smoke, the blood is being pumped through the body at an increased rate. Smoking has a detrimental domino effect on not only our bodies but our egos. Fatty deposits are laid down on the walls of the blood vessels more rapidly, narrowing them and causing them to lose their elasticity, driving the pressure higher and increasing the taxation on the heart further. High blood pressure results, which makes us more prone to anger and irritation. We are more impatient than we would be without the poison in our system.[1]

Our whole life is different than it would be if we didn't

smoke. Our egos will attempt to take care of all the side effects smoking brings. We may even develop defense mechanisms in our personality to try to check the guilt we are carrying. One good example of this is the closet smoker.

The closet smoker is a fairly recent guilt-ridden paranoid phenomenon. Until the eighties people quit out of concern for their health alone. These days smoking in public can be just about as embarrassing as wearing a hair shirt to the town square and publicly flogging oneself. So the closet smoker has developed a layer of affectations upon the affectations already acquired by being just a plain old smoker.

I remember when I was a closet smoker. On top of the original paranoia that smoking might kill me I then had to *hide* the thing that was killing me. I felt like the keeper of a dirty secret. And there were things I had to remember.

I had to remember to clean and hide my ashtrays. The threat of discovery hovered constantly . . . "Oh, say, what's this here behind *Crime and Punishment* on your bookshelf? . . . a cigarette in an ashtray? Who's been smoking it? You're not still smoking are you?"

When I was driving the car I had to remember to keep the cigarette below window level, just in case somebody I knew was in the lane beside me. This was especially true at stop lights where I couldn't slow down or speed up but was a sitting duck, and even if the cigarette *was* hidden there was all that smoke pouring out the window.

It was also important not to leave any telltale signs in the car ashtray. At first this forced me to commit the illegal act of throwing my burning butts out the window. Then I got smart. I made a convenient portable ashtray I could carry under the front seat of my car. It was a simple, cheap homemade device, one small mason jar with a half inch of water covering the bottom. The airtight lid prevented the odor from leaking out. If you are a closet smoker and you want to try this, just make sure the jar doesn't roll out from under the seat while you're driving with a friend who doesn't know you're still smoking.

For a while I was a pretty weird Houdini with the slights of hand I performed. Once in a while one hand forgot what the other hand was doing. That was because of the stress of always having something to hide.

Smoke is hard to hide. You can't put it in your pocket, stuff it under the bed or the couch, put it in your purse, slam your book shut on it, swat it or shoo it out of the house. Many closet smokers thought at first it was this visible smoke they had to hide only to find that their lovers and friends knew all along because of the smell.

When my guilt became too much to bear I even fantasized that I had quit smoking. I went so far as to pretend around my friends that I had quit. I would then be the first to leave a party so that I could have a smoke on the way home, retrieving the pack hidden behind everything else in the glove compartment.

We who have become closet smokers don't literally smoke in a closet. I smoked in my car, on walks (at night), on the back step. I smoked standing in the bathtub and blew the smoke out the window. Because of the telltale odor of smoke I had a smoking hat so that no one could smell it on my hair. Whenever I wanted a cigarette I would put on my smoking hat and sit on my back step or go for my nightly phantom smoker walks ducking behind this tree, that bush whenever one of the neighbors passed into view. In my pocket was my smoker's breath freshener kit: A colorful selection of Sen Sens, Doublemint gum, cough drops, lifesavers—depending on my mood.

14 The Land of the Living

During the course of the flu I'd hardly eaten more than a cup of soup every twenty-four hours. The day I stuck my big toe back into the world again, I felt as weak and holy as a saint coming off the desert of a two week fast. I felt what it feels like to not have the rivers of my body polluted with chemical waste products and empty beer cans.

I was detoxified! And pleasantly surprised to find myself less angry at the world in general. My body felt joyous, exhilarated. My body felt like it had found a buried treasure. I was no longer restless, but content to just sit and look out the window of Mr. Toots at the ocean. I remembered the anti-smoking ads I'd seen on television in the sixties of people jumping up and down and clicking their heels. That's exactly how I felt.

I glowed. People were looking at me differently. Smiling. That's because I was smiling. My battery had a positive charge and my eyes were on "bright." My skin had cleared up. I laughed more. I thought about different things or, rather, differently about the same things. My flesh had risen from the dead and I could feel the air circulating through the pores of my skin which was breathing where once it was just a limp encasement for my thoughts and emotions. If my life was a trilogy, the third part had just begun. Along with this third volume of my life a third part of me, myself, the "I", was coming alive. I had come off the desert of withdrawal.

It was time to start writing again. I took out the script I'd been working on before I quit smoking. I put some paper in the typewriter on my desk. I sat down in front of it. And sat. And sat. About twenty minutes into the sitting I realized I was paralyzed. You could have held a cashier's check for one million dollars in front of my nose and told me it was mine if I typed four coherent pages—but I would not have been able to do it. For two hours I sat staring at the blank page in my typewriter.

It was during these two hours that I realized the importance of paper for the first time. Since paper is part of the writer's paraphernalia, this was a revelation akin to Galileo discovering gravity.

Paper may be the most important invention of mankind. More and more our future depends on paper and the information and images we put on it. Imagine what the world would be like if paper had never been invented. We would have more trees. There would be no post offices. No libraries. No recorded history. The Declaration of Independence would have been merely thought or else it would have been written on a rock. Advertising would be etched by airplanes in the sky.

Then again if we didn't have so much paper we probably wouldn't have so much to advertise. This is because paper magnifies our importance. It is a mirror for our thoughts that not only preserves them but allows us to perpetuate and multiply our ideas like rabbits.

The success of cigarettes probably depended more on paper than the tobacco itself. They were first promoted with paper cards—baseball and pin-up cards of actresses to lure the "common man." They were advertised in magazines made of paper and on billboards pasted over with paper. The first cigarettes were rolled in newspaper. Next they were packaged ten to a paper box by East European Jews who worked ten hours a day rolling them by hand. Each one turned out approximately three thousand cigarettes a shift. (Three hundred an hour. Five every minute. One every twelve seconds.)

Another item made out of paper, about the length of a pin, that has long gone unheralded for the role it has played in the widespread use of cigarettes, is the match. Certainly the match outranks the ashtray and breath mint in the smoker's paraphernalia kit. Have you ever wondered why we never see matches advertised? They don't have to be. Advertising is for products that are in competition with each other and describe for us the utilitarian uses or "aesthetic" designs that make one item better or more appealing than another. A match is a match. Like bobby pins, screws, paper clips, staples, they are necessary items. They don't need to be promoted. They don't need to be decorated. Why bother to spruce up something that is designed to self-destruct as soon as you use it?

Behind every cigarette there is a match. The Indians of America, Europe and Africa used the drilling method (hands twirling a tapered stick in a shallow wood pit) to make fire. It was the development of the match, the humblest of all commodities, that made it possible for smokers to light up more than the Indians ever did. These little fire sticks changed an entertaining practice which one might have indulged in three times a day into a physical dependency some now crave sixty times a day.

The modest match broadened the smokers' horizons so they could smoke any time anywhere—unless they wanted to go swimming. In the first era of the safe match cigarette users doubled their consumption to ten a day. Manufacturers started supplying them (gratefully) twenty to a pack before the end of the 1880s.

Matches weren't always as harmless as they are now. In the 1890s, gentlemen didn't carry matches in their pockets anymore than they would have a loaded gun. Early attempts at making phosphoric matches were dangerous because, on occasion, they lit too readily, and the white phosphorous caused serious disease among the workers who made them. Before tobacco was known to be dangerous to your health, the white phosphorus used in matches was thought to cause tuberculosis. Cigars were lit from the cinders of existing fires. Cigar stores had gas lamps upon which their customers could light up. The decision to light a cigar entailed forethought, and they were never chain-smoked like cigarettes.

Greeks and Romans used tapers tipped with sulfur and animal fats which could be lit—if the air was warm enough and not too wet. The Greek god Prometheus was tortured for giving man fire, and this curse seems to have followed the fire-stick makers throughout history. One inventor in particular stands out. The German, I.F. Kammerer, created the first match that friction could ignite. But he was forbidden by the German Confederation to both make and sell these "dangerous contrivances." When he attempted to sell his matches he was discovered by the government. All his equipment was destroyed, his property taken away and he was punished severely. After this he went mad and died in an asylum at Ludwigsburg.[1]

Seventeenth century France and Germany had "tinder pistols" that employed flints and gunpowder. If the timing slipped, which it often did, there would be an explosion. Late in the eighteenth century, some French inventors came up with "phosphorus candles"—phosphorus-soaked paper in a glass tube. When the tube was crushed, the paper would burst into flames.[2] Next came the Italians' cheap version called the "pocket luminary." This was a bottle lined with phosphorus oxide. It was kept tightly sealed. When you wanted fire, you would open the bottle and rub a sulfur-tipped splint against the interior of the bottle. But if you didn't remove this quickly there was a good chance the bottle would blow up in your hands.

A Joke

How many Italians does it take to light a match?
ANSWER: Ten. One to light it, three to take him to the hospital and six to pick the glass out of the carpets and walls.

◆   ◆   ◆

Although Joshua Pusey was not Italian, he could have been an Italian joke. He used a cardboard instead of wooden splints and was the first to contain matches in a book. Each of these books had fifty matches just like those of today. Unfortunately, his invention proved a failure technologically and for a ridiculously simple reason: the striking surface was on the *inside* of the book instead of the *outside*. Sparks created by the friction of striking the match ignited the remaining forty-nine matches. A mere gnat in the eye of the giant, but for some odd reason Pusey wasn't able to see how easily his problem could be solved. He sold his invention to Diamond in 1885 and his relatives are still cursing him today.[3]

15   Writers and Quitting

I owe to smoking more or less, in life the whole of my success; . . . when smoking all my ideas soar, when not they sink upon the floor.

ANONYMOUS

I found I could not put any words on paper without smoking. I wanted to take a puff, lay the cigarette down in the ashtray, blow the smoke out of my mouth as I typed a paragraph, pick up the cigarette, take a puff. Without cigarettes writing wasn't going to be fun anymore. "You are not alone in this problem," I told myself.

Many writers smoked throughout history, in fact, *most*. Once Tennyson traveled to Italy but left his party of companions at their hotel and went back home again when he found out that his favorite brand of tobacco wasn't sold anywhere nearby. Mark Twain followed a strict discipline: he never smoked at meals or while asleep. Ben Jonson always had snuff dust on his waistcoat and upper lip. Dickens smoked.

Some writers didn't smoke. When Saki lay dying in a trench during the First World War, his last words were, "Put that bloody cigarette out!"[1]

Eventually, the absence of typewriter keys clacking was a burden on my shoulders, my fingers, my brain. The hum of the electric typewriter was a command I couldn't obey. I felt inadequate. I felt like a soldier who'd gone AWOL during a *good* war. The white sheet of paper was Outer Siberia and I was the condemned prisoner fated to wander forever in search of ideas.

What was I going to do? Kill myself after all? Go back to smoking? "Just smoke while you write!" the Throat Monster (who I thought I'd killed) spoke up from his grave.

"NO!" I typed on the page in front of me. I would like to say this was the beginning of my writing again, but it wasn't. And the longer I sat there, the more did the great negative NO! before me come to stand for an answer, a universal resolve that NO! I was not going to find a way out of this one! So I typed, "Oh *YES*, I will! I will! I will! I Will!"

I made a plan. The only way to climb a mountain is to crawl up inch by inch. I decided that I would go to Mr. Toots every morning and drink a Borgia (the best cup of coffee in the world) while I wrote. Instead of a cigarette, the coffee would be my reward. Mr. Toots was the only cafe in town that doesn't allow smoking. It would have been too surreal to have other people blowing smoke all around me. Like quitting sugar and going to work for See's Candies. Besides, in all the other cafes there were too many people not interested in work. Santa Cruz is the kind of tourist town where even the residents seem to be on a perpetual vacation. The cafes are always crowded with locals who never seem to have anything to do or anywhere else to go, as if they had recently been dropped down from the sky.

The first day I drove to Capitola at 8:00 in the morning, the same hour most people in the world go to work. I walked into the cafe with my notebook and pen and sat down at a table by the window, ready to write. Unfortunately, my brain refused to focus at all. I sat at the table next to the window looking out at the ocean and the sailboats anchored near the wharf. I watched the sea gulls hovering around the deck of Mr. Toots as if it were a fishing boat. I watched Georgianne, a ravenous local seagull, who was sitting on the railing peering back at me through the window where she waited to be fed a croissant or, perhaps, a pitcher of cream. For two hours I watched this bird. On my second workday I sat down in the same spot and refused to take my eyes off the blank page in front of me. I wrote at the top of the page, in the scrawly letters of a third-grader, *Robotville, Anywhere Earth Orb.*

I wrote this title down because I thought I was going to work on the movie script I'd been fiddling around with before I'd quit smoking. Instead I found myself writing (theoretically) about how hard it was to write. It was so hard to write without a cigarette that I only wrote about not being able to write for fifteen minutes that first day. The next day I doubled my time. Each day following I added fifteen minutes so that within a week I was back writing two hours at a stretch. Here is the first "piece" I completed after quitting cigarettes and, if this book had opened at its actual conception in time, this is where it would have begun chronologically:

Why the Cigarette is
Mightier than the Pen

When a writer quits smoking, there is not only the loss of a friend (the cigarette who is now your enemy), but the absence of writing. My mind boycotts work. It is on a sit-down strike. My brain refuses to synthesize, to process, to follow any idea to its logical conclusion. My brain is a bowl of alphabet soup.

With the exception of gamblers and mechanics, the occupation of writing probably has the most smokers. Why? Because the cigarette is the same shape as a crayon, pencil, pen. A writer who smokes cannot help but associate cigarettes with these other tools of the trade until they become just as important as the sound of the typewriter tapping and the scratching of the pencil revising. They all go together like notes in a song, and if one element is taken out, the beat falters, you trip over your words, you stutter every time you try to sing.

The feel of the cigarette between my fingers while I write was long ago grafted onto my thinking process and into the sentences I put down on paper. Not having it here is like taking the shoo out of the bop shoo bop, the doo out of the doo wah diddy. By repeatedly associating the cigarette in my hand with what I was writing, a misinterpretation took place and an incorrect message was sent to my brain which said, "Smoking is the exercise of the creator. When you have ideas, it is because you are smoking."

Abra cadabra. The cigarette was no longer just along for the ride, but became the magic wand bringing forth the work; the fuel for my muse. I was the little engine that thinks it can, puff puff puffing to get the work accomplished. Typical of the victim, I gave away my power to another source.

Most smokers have many aspects in their jobs not associated with cigarettes. Writers write. They cannot run away to other people or to a task unrelated to smoking. It's harder for a writer to quit because he fears he will never be able to write (not to mention enjoy writing) again. Too much is being lost at once, smoking and one's occupation.

◆   ◆   ◆

Writing the above led me into writing my true confessions as a smoker, the mental purge that turned out to be the beginning of this book. After a month of writing about my life as a smoker, I told myself I might as well turn it into a book. After all, I had read by now most of the books that have been written on smoking.

But any progress I had gained while writing about my life as a smoker was lost once my brain knew I was going to turn it into a book. The gears froze again. "Book? She's writing a *book*? Oh no. I can't do that. No no no. That's *work*!" So I fooled my brain. I brought a foot high stack of smoke books with me to the cafe every day and merely *scanned* them. I took *simple* notes on what I thought was interesting. I told my brain, "No harm here. See, we're just plagiarizing! We're not really *writing*." If I'd been a painter quitting smoking, I would have had tracing paper over a Rembrandt.

My thinking process was learning how to walk all over again. I was hoping my brain would hitchhike a ride on the pure emulation of it all. I was teasing forth thought. It worked. Within several days my brain was taking those first few awkward steps alone; little spasmodic fragments of ideas that it had thought of all by itself. I was careful to pretend I hadn't noticed and continued copying modestly. The ideas for how to construct this book came out—one, two, three steps . . . fall down, get up . . . one, two, three . . . god I wish I could smoke a cigarette.

They came out erratically because in retaliation for me making it go back to work, my brain had decided to capriciously toss my thoughts like confetti into the air. Catch 'em if you can! My job for the first month was to write them down as they came out randomly, sporadically, straggling, vague, as unattached to each other as they were to the syntax of their own tribes: sentences had beginnings and no endings, direct objects were mere innuendoes, paragraphs belonged to a future century. After I wrote them down I had a lot of these little pieces which I had to put together like one of those giant jigsaw puzzles you buy of the Sierra Nevada.

Five weeks later the fits and starts had subsided and my brain was forming whole paragraphs. The fifteen-minute span of attention had stretched to two hours during which I nursed my goblet of Borgia as if it were gold. Within a month I was ready to go to Mr. Toots *twice* a day. I was working for four hours, a stint in the morning and another in the afternoon. This was not a cafe to me now but an office. I figured my monthly table rent at about one hundred and twenty dollars—two Borgias a day at one dollar and seventy-five cents each and two twenty-five cent tips. One hundred and twenty dollars a month for coffee! Next year I can write a book about quitting caffeine.

16   The Bewitcher

"Few if any industries in America offer such a glowing testimonial to the power of advertising."

HARRY WOOTEN

*I*n the 1980s freedom has come to mean the ability to make our lives glamourous. This is why we are so vulnerable to advertisers. More than ever, advertisers are the wizards, prophets, poets and kings. Their time has arrived. They specialize in glamour.

The survival of the fittest now means who can use his brain to catch the most consumers. Ad men are the modern day wolves chasing us rabbits through meadows of promises. Our wolves know where to bite us and it is in the same wishful thinking place that originally created myths. Ad men know the power our wishful thoughts have over us. They know we are as hypnotized by promises that will alleviate our fears of ugliness, impotency, illness and poverty just as we were once hypnotized by the god myths.

The first thing to understand about the advertising man is that he is a professional liar—unless there are some very stupid people out there who really believe cigarettes are "mild as May."

Cigarettes do not sell the same way most commodities do—ice cream, aspirin, Mr. Clean—the things one uses once in a while. Most things aren't highly addictive in the sense that we would get down on our hands and knees in the gutter looking for them, as I and at least ten other smokers that I know have done.

The cigarette ad men are a special breed. They know full well that once they've got us hooked on nicotine we are likely to become lifetime customers, i.e., addicts. Like pushers, they make their living from our addiction. Motivated to hook us, they'll even pass out free cigarettes on the street corners (four to a pack) acting like they're doing us a favor. When a teenager takes to cigarettes the ad men know that he will be a customer for the next fifty years or so, unless he dies from them first. Every teenager is potentially 18,700 packs of cigarettes.

This is the reason cigarette companies spend $1.5 billion a year to advertise in newspapers, magazines and billboards. Between 1971 and 1981 *Cosmopolitan* published 8 articles on smoking and 155 articles on dieting. Ten percent of its revenue came from cigarette ads. During the same ten years neither *Redbook* nor *Ms.* (16% and 14% revenue from the ads, respectively) ran a single article specifically on smoking.[1]

Both *Cosmopolitan* and *Psychology Today* refused to run ads for a national chain of anti-smoking clinics. When interviewed on TV's 20/20 an ad executive from *Cosmopolitan* said, "We *can't* accept it. We get 200 pages of cigarette advertising (a year) . . . am I going to jeopardize $5 to $10 million worth of business?"[2]

One wonders what the cigarette ad men are like in their daily lives. What kind of homes do they come from? Were their fathers traveling salesmen who told them the moon was made of green cheese? Many endorsements for ads have been fakes. Constance Talmadge became a standing joke when she posed in and endorsed eleven different products in an October 29, 1927 issue of *Liberty Magazine*. Queen Marie of Romania consented to so many ads she was laughed at. It was well known that many famous people endorsed products they didn't use. In the twenties Madame Schumann-Heink, a European opera singer, took back her endorsement for Luckies because she felt she'd been exploited.[3]

Printer's Ink ran a story about a football player who took $4,000 for a cigarette testimonial, "notwithstanding the fact the he has never smoked and admitted that he couldn't discriminate between the aroma of a burning mattress and a dollar Perfecto." Lucky Strikes got a testimonial from Captain George Fried who had recently made the newspaper headlines for a rescue-at-sea mission. Later it was reported that he smoked Old Golds. Afterward he lost out on a deal with that company for twice as much money.[4]

What cigarette ads have always done is try to get us hooked by associating royalty, aristocracy, wealth, power and sexual success with smoking tobacco. But of course they couldn't show us the truth: a bunch of bums sorting through the garbage, fish heads strewn around their feet, cotton swabs stuck to their frayed coats, chunks of stale bread sticking out of their pockets—passing around a cigarette butt.

It would be an interesting experiment to see if people would keep smoking if the names for popular cigarettes were changed overnight to things like Hogs Breath and Turkey Shit. We then might see how gullible we've been under the power of the written word and the image.

No one is ever going to be able to prove statistically, down to the wire, just how much the ads have affected us. Probably no one has said to himself, "Yes, it was definitely the day I saw that ad where the man and woman lit up in front of a fire on a bear skin rug and she had on a gold sequined dress that I lit my first cigarette."

Ads don't so much tempt us into getting hooked as they do legitimize the act through an unconscious association. After we are hooked, they reinforce the idea that smoking is OK. Ads make it easier for us to smoke. Even though the twelve-feet tall people on the billboards aren't *real* people, still, they influence us. Why? Because they are bigger than we are! And they are always *up there.* They are one constant in an inconstant world. We forget that they have nothing else to do but be there. They, unlike us, do not have a home to go to. They will be posing there forever. And, even though there is no logic in their message aimed at our brain, the idea that these nice-looking people would rather smoke cigarettes than do anything else (because they are always smoking when we pass them by) becomes locked into our minds. Sure it doesn't make any sense, but this is how the robot programming part of us works. Surely, people like these models . . . so handsome, beautiful, seemingly intelligent by their choices of clothing, hairstyles, the Rolex on their wrists, their looks of glowing health, their measured gazes, the library books behind them on the shelf in the den . . . (Look! There's *Walden* by Thoreau!) . . . surely these models have had many choices in life. They could have been airplane pilots, lawyers, teachers; but every time we look at them, the thing they seem to have chosen to do is to smoke a cigarette.

Perhaps evolution has taken a kinky twist and has us standing in front of a mirror with our images grabbing hold of us by the necks and trading places with us. Ads are to us what Narcissus' pool was to him (and we know what happened to him, he fell in and drowned). In them we can see our own images, whether of thought or body, reflected so that we can dwell and ponder on what we see there. Perhaps we would rather be photographs?

At present we are dangerously close to becoming photographs and we may be on the cutting edge of the Age of the Photograph. If we can project this concept further into the future, the succeeding era will be the Age of the Negative, seeing as how we seem to be reversing ourselves. A metamorphosis almost as horrible as Kafka's character who woke up one morning to find himself transformed into a cockroach.

Are we now mere paper dolls defining outselves by somebody else's image of us? Never before has fashion changed as often as it now does, whether in clothing, cars, interior decorations, or music. And that is why the advertiser has learned to cast a wide net. The best example of this is the cigarette ad that shows this turkey standing in front of a four wheel drive Cherokee. He is the natural man, without the sweat. His skin is dark (not too dark, well tanned), he is bearded (but well clipped), he is young (but not too young), dressed in a khaki shirt and pants (tailored). He has a comb sticking out of his breast pocket. There it is, the *gold chain*! He's even got a couple of pendants hanging on the end of the chain. Are they medals? For fighting in a war? The Olympics? Is he a debating champion? Chess?

Here we have the classic example of the homogenized hype media image. They leave the associations as wide as possible so a lot of people can identify with the picture. Why, with his caterpillar mustache, this guy could even be a San Francisco gay.

So much for the accessories, what about the *inner* man? By his direct gaze we can assume he is straightforward and probably honest (unless he makes drug runs in the Cherokee. Say, what *does* he use the jeep for? Is he a surveyor? Does he work with Indians? Does he use it to check on oil wells? Is he a Texas Ranger?)

The words in quotes at the bottom of his photograph are like the captions we put in our photograph albums under the pictures we take of our friends, "Bob says there's nothing like watermelon at a picnic." Except the turkey is saying, "If I'm going to smoke, I'm going to do it right." Of course, if he was our friend and we had taken this photo of him, we would have captioned it, "If I'm going to get cancer, I'm going to do it by smoking the brand I like."

But Winston isn't going to fork out a million bucks to have him say that. Instead, the caption continues and he says, "Some people smoke a brand for its image. I don't. You can't taste image." *This* from somebody who is so involved with what he looks like he hasn't a hair out of place on his head. The punch line? "Winston is for real."

Who *is* this guy? Where is he right now? How many other guys are out there like this one? How many really believe that this stereotype represents the heart and soul of what it means to be an adventurer? This guy is what all the conformists think it would look like to be their own man.

Since most of us don't pursue rugged individualism by straying too far afield from the flock, we find our other possible selves in the ads. The ad becomes a gestalt. Here is the Greek drama condensed for modern man into the quickie catharsis. While waiting at a stoplight we are purged of our wild untameable desires for adventure and sex in a five-second billboard transference. The billboards and magazine pictures, wilder all the time (in exact relation to how controlled we become) provide us with a psychological necessity. As the world continues to shrink and corporate culture continues to lariat us, as the mysteries of life get blocked off on computer screens, our adventures locked up in keyboards, we confuse what we wear with what we feel and we begin to feel best if what we wear is autographed by its designer. This way we feel more authentic. It's like owning a Picasso instead of a print.

Of course if we could exist in the ads, if we could live in the movies, then we would never have to quit smoking! Or, perhaps, if we put on a pair of jeans with the designer's name on them we might mold our bodies into works of art that are immortal.

◆   ◆   ◆

I had been living a vicarious life for many years before I came out of my photograph. Fantasy goes well with smoking. In this photograph I was sitting on the couch staring off into space at the smoke curling upward or watching my own hand writing. When I finally quit smoking I became a moving object that pushed the dominos now in a positive direction.

First of all I found that exercise gave me relief whenever cigarette nostalgia struck. So I bought a mountain bike. This bike was so expensive I needed to buy a Kryptonite lock so nobody would steal it. I rode this bike out of the self-imposed exile of my photograph straight into the people dimension.

I joined a health spa where I saw . . . more people. After I joined the spa I purchased workout clothes and a pair of Reeboks, so I wouldn't wreck my body before I tenderized it on the exercise floor. Having just spent a small fortune on the spa I felt I should utilize it, so I joined an aerobics class where I met . . . more people.

I estimate that I spent twelve hundred dollars (plus tax). I have spent much more than that on cigarettes in my life. If I had opted to buy twelve hundred packs of cigarettes instead (at a pack per day) they would have lasted me over three years. The spa membership only lasts two years. Still, I got the best deal. The mountain bike lasts a lot longer than that. And if I should get myself into terrific shape maybe I'll meet a millionaire on one of my bike rides and end up marrying him.

Just as once I was driven back into a closet, now I was driven to be around other people in order to soothe the loneliness that cigarettes once put off. Especially at night.

My sister probably benefitted from my neurotic social needs during this time more than anyone else. Usually I appeared at her doorstep around supper time. After a few weeks of good meals I had to begin making myself useful. I played with my nephew, Stefan, while she cooked dinner. I folded clothes. Gave Stefan a bath. Changed his diapers. Put his pajamas on him. Fixed his bottle. Told him his bedtime story. Then, after he went to sleep, I did the dishes. Inevitably there would come the point in the evening when my sister would yawn, my brother-in-law would mention what a long day it had been and they would go off to bed together leaving me vacuuming or, perhaps, dusting, saying to them, "You guys go on to bed. I'll be finishing up here in a few minutes."

17   Back to the Garbage Can

"Hill would have known what to do about this cancer business," one Madison Avenue ad man said. "He would have made cancer fashionable."

*I*n the late 1950s in *Rebel Without a Cause*, James Dean showed cigarette smoking for what it is, a nervous habit one seeks consolation in yet does not find. By the mid-sixties our movie heroes weren't smoking as much. Humphrey Bogart died of lung cancer. Elvis Presley carried a guitar instead of a cigarette. Annette Funicello and Frankie Avalon played volleyball on the beach. Peace, love and health began to be issues. A shift had taken place. The upper class, originally the last to take on smoking, began to quit.

Jack Lemmon, Tony Randall and Tony Curtis made commercials against smoking. While playing Hamilton Burger on the TV Series "Perry Mason," William Talman came down with lung cancer. Perilously close to death, he told the TV audience in his commercial, "I have lung cancer. Take some advice about smoking and losing from someone who's been doing both for years. If you haven't smoked—don't start. If you do smoke—quit. Don't be a loser."[1] Talman died before the commercial reached the air, which gave his statement more impact than the Surgeon General's announcement that smoking may be hazardous to your health.

In the fifties Edward R. Murrow smoked cigarettes on television while presenting the news. But in the seventies we knew Johnny Carson smoked during commercials only because once in a while the camera caught him off-guard taking a drag.

The last televised cigarette commercial was aired on both radio and television before midnight, January 1, 1971. Pulling the plug didn't stop the cigarette companies from trying to out-maneuver us again, however. "Well, what would Father Bernays have done in our position?" they probably asked each other. "Sponsor gatherings that will *unconsciously* link us with valuable qualities like sports and art." Suddenly "events" in the classic Bernays style kept popping up out of nowhere in unexpected places. News-making events such as fashion shows, concerts and art festivals.

Slick attempts were made to get back on the airwaves in front of the "crowd" by Philip Morris when it sponsored a television tennis tournament named after its new cigarette, Virginia Slims. Then it took in the Marlboro Australia Open, Marlboro British Grand Prix, Marlboro Cup Horse Races. R.J. Reynolds sponsored the pro soccer team, Team America, the World Cup Soccer Championship, Camel Ski Days, Camel Expeditions Wilderness Safaris, Western Rodeo Series, International Hot Rod Association, American Motorcycle Association. Let us not forget the Lucky Strikes Darts Tournament, the Kool Jazz Festival and, the ultimate in hypocrisy, Raleigh's Children's Cancer Classic Celebrity Golf Tournament.

Philip Morris paid a small fortune to have Marlboros used in *Superman II*. In her publicity photos Lois Lane smoked them. The logo appears approximately twenty-four times on the screen. Marlboro had more than a cameo role.[2]

Now, instead of riding in on a black horse, the bad guy slinks in with a cigarette between his lips. The good guys don't go near cigarettes in movies anymore. Telly Savalas played Theo Kojak, a cop who kicked the smoking habit by sucking on a lollipop.

It was way back in 1966 that all cigarette packages had to begin carrying a label stating "Caution—Cigarette Smoking May Be Hazardous To Your Health." But the government had too much pressure from the tobacco industry to do little more than pay lip service to the facts. On the "Today Show" in 1978, Joseph Califano, the Secretary of Health, Education and Welfare, declared plans to spend millions in advertising the health problems caused by smoking, that he wanted a higher tax per pack and that he wanted to get rid of smoking sections on passenger planes. The White House was informed of the "speech" a half an hour before air-time. And when asked about the anti-smoking speech the White House staff hemmed and hawed over the aforementioned measures saying, finally, that Califano's ideas weren't President Carter's.[3]

Any president has a lot to lose from such a campaign and a southern president has even more to lose. Califano was not only ignored by the administration he worked for, he was crucified by the press. "Joe gave up smoking two-and-a-half-years ago. Now that he's seen the light, he insists that no one else asks for one."[4] "Isn't there something else Joe ought to be doing, now that he's got his wind back? Aren't there a few wrinkles left in the welfare program, near perfect as it is?"[5] Poor St. Joe. A few years ahead of his time.

Dr. Peter Bourne, President Carter's Special Assistant for Health Issues, had already spoken out against a public ban on smoking. "There is a small minority of people who have a hypersensitivity to smoke. We cannot write the laws to protect this small group, overlooking a much larger group who are entitled to the same basic rights."[6]

By 1984 Califano still hadn't succeeded in banning smoking from public places. I know because *I* was still smoking in public places. One night after a good meal at India Joze, a late hour Indonesian cuisine restaurant, my friends and I were talking about water pollution. As I let the smoke drift from my mouth the way it does out the exhaust of a car idling, I said something like, "I wonder how long underground springs can go uncontaminated?"

One of the men seated in a group at the next table laughed out loud. Then he said to his companions, "People who smoke publicly are invading the rights of others to breathe fresh air!" As he spoke he stared at my cigarette. "This invasionary smoke has two times as much tar and nicotine, three times as much Benzpyrene, fifty times as much ammonia and much more *cadmium* than polluted air." What was he, the American Cancer Society's main man? Somewhere between the Benzpyrene and the cadmium I put the burning cigarette out in my glass of water.

"What's Benzpyrene?" one of my companions nudged me—I guess because I had been the only one smoking. I didn't know the answer. Shame-faced, I watched the water turning yellow as the absorbent cigarette grew to the proportions of a small cigar. I didn't look up once even as the paper uncurled, burst apart, sent the poison particles spurting forth.

My public smoking was snuffed out for good. It wasn't until I was doing research for this book two years later that I found out some more facts about cigarette smoke: 1. Benzpyrene is a cancer-producing substance and cigarette smoke contains one million times *more* particles of it than does polluted air. 2. The concentration of hydrogen cyanide—you know, the deadly gas used in gas chambers—in cigarette smoke is sixteen hundred parts per million. 3. A non-smoker breaths in the equivalent of one cigarette when in a closed room in which ten cigarettes are smoked. 4. Smokers in America alone send nearly forty tons of solid air pollution in the form of tobacco smoke into the sky each day. 5. There is about the same amount of carbon monoxide in cigarette smoke as there is in automobile exhaust.[7]

Whether or not Califano is a saint is not the issue. The

reason Califano didn't have backup in his crusade against cigarettes is because they are a $60-billion-a-year industry. Cigarettes account for 2.5 percent of the gross national product.[8] Cigarette money not only controls the government, it controls the media. Even magazines that run articles against smoking run cigarette ads alongside them.

For the last fourteen years Norway has banned cigarette advertising. What responsibility does our media owe to its "crowd" of readers? It will be up to the public to change the value quality of the ads. When bicycles are prized more highly than cigarettes, then the bicycle companies will be able to afford expensive ads.

While anti-cigarette forces continued to stress the connection between cigarettes and illness, the cigarette ads danced over, under, sideways, down by appealing to things that had nothing to do with cigarettes such as humor, nature, and relationships. Perhaps the best ad foolery of them all was when the cigarette companies attempted to keep women smoking by riding the bandwagon of feminism.

It should have been the title to a good novel about women coming into their own. Or a quote from Gloria Steinem. A line in a poem by Alice Walker. What a shame for history that the words "You've Come A Long Way, Baby!" were publicized by cigarette advertisers. I can just hear the ad men at their table, "Why, we're part of the movement! We're helping them attain equality with men!"

Time Magazine ran an article in February, 1986, about the first "designer cigarette," whose brand logo is Frances Yves Saint Laurent. Sally MacKinnon, obviously a pseudo-liberated female V.P. of R.J. Reynolds, said in an interview that these newer 100mm cigarettes were for women who were "more independent, probably tending to be single rather than married, and who spend more of their income on fashion and fashion accessories."[9]

Women smokers are on the rise even as they are rising in

the ranks. Are women, in their newly found freedoms, merely taking over the males' roles? The male identity? Is our addiction to a male-oriented society that strong? To get a Prince Charming you've got to be charming princess who does not have the smell of tobacco on your lips when he wants to kiss you. What kind of man wants his woman to smoke? A man who smokes, of course.

Where once cigarette ads projected an "upper class" look, now they went for the health inference by appealing to the "natural woman." And who is more natural than the *first* woman, Eve? The ad has her in the Garden of Eden wearing a blouse made with the same design as is printed on the cigarette pack and the filter: paisley green, like a forest floor. As if cigarettes were themselves the direct route back to the Garden of Eden, back to innocence, back to health itself.

But the ads weren't working like they used to. Tobacco addicts were going AWOL left and right. What were the cigarette companies going to do to keep insurrection in the ranks at bay? They simply joined the other side and in the blink of an eye there was no more battle. The cigarette companies put on the costumes of the Cigarette Red Cross and marched in disguised as More, Waterford, True, Now, Merit with their life saving low tars and nicotines. They ignored the fact that the filters on many cigarettes contain even more dangerous substances than tobacco. Also, though light tar and nicotine cigarettes might result in less cancer they give you more carbon monoxide and hence, more emphysema.

These last efforts by the cigarette companies to keep us hooked symbolized perfectly the symbiotic victim-savior relationship. "Let me save you so you will remain a victim and I can keep getting my power from you."

A bird in the hand is worth two hopping out into the bush. Fewer smokers and greater organized opposition to smoking gave the cigarette companies a good reason to diversify their interests. They bought as many consumer-oriented products as they could handle. They already had the ability to create products, advertise them and then market them effectively. So they not only bought other manufacturing companies, they bought the packaging companies and the transit operations. What had once been used to create and sell cigarettes would now be used to sell consumer goods such as gum, razors, shaving cream, wine, soda and beer. Once the major addiction is threatened, what else but go to the minor ones?

In 1960 Philip Morris bought out American Safety Razor, then Burma Vita, Clark Gum and several small hospital-supply operations (to take care of the growing lung cancer patients?) In 1968, they obtained majority control of Miller Brewing Company. Then they went into land development and dabbled in Australian wines. In 1978 they acquired Seven-Up.[10]

Reynolds bought Pacific Hawaiian Products (Hawaiian Punch, etc.), Penick & Ford (Brer Rabbit and Vermont Maid Syrups, My-T-Fine desserts, among other food products). Then it acquired petroleum companies and packaging companies and spent $200 million for McLean Industries, the leader in containerized freight.

In 1966 American Tobacco bought Sunshine Biscuits and Jim Beam Distilling Company. Two years later, they bought Bell Brand Foods and Duffy- Mott, and in 1970 they took over Swingline, a manufacturer of office equipment along with Acme Visible Records, Master Lock and the cosmetic company of Andrew Jergen. Lorillard (Kent) went into candy and cat food.

L&M already owned Allen Products, the canner of Alpo Dog Food. Next they dove straight into the liquor field. If they could create ads to get us to drink, perhaps we'd smoke more? They purchased Paddington, the importer of J&B Scotch, Bombay Gin, and other leading brands. In 1966 they bought Star Industries, a liquor distributor.[11]

Like a phoenix rising from its ashes, the cigarette companies learned how to survive their own extinction.

As have we. Now cigarettes are banned from most public places such as shopping malls, theatres, restaurants. Ten years ago health problems caused by smoking cigarettes hardly made the newspapers. Now it is to the headlines we look to see what direction smoking is taking: Survey Finds 18 Million Join In Great American Smokeout . . . Move Toward A "Smoke-Free" U.S. Gains Steadily . . . Singapore Sets Sights On "Smoke-Free" Goal . . . Jersey Seeks Tighter Curbs On Smoking. . . The Most Addictive Drug . . . Lung Cancer Is Expected To Become Top Killer Of Women . . . Harmful Habit: Cigarette Smoking Is Growing Hazardous To Careers In Business.[12]

Where once it was assumed smokers could light up whenever and wherever they wanted, now it is the reverse and probably no headline could say it better than the one in the *New York Times* on April 9, 1985, which read, "Smokers Have Rights, Too."[13]

Wrapping It Up:
Will I Ever Go Back?

What began here as a purely mechanical exercise to help me write without smoking has since turned into a book. The afternoon I finished I got up from the table (at Toots, of course) and went out to the deck. As I stood at the railing I discovered that my brain, originally reluctant to begin this project, was now just as reluctant to end it. The pistons were still churning, "like a phoenix rising from its ashes . . . like a phoenix rising from its ashes . . ."

"O.K. You can stop now," I told it. "Don't worry, we'll begin a new book soon."

". . . like a phoenix . . ."

To distract myself from this phase-out stage I looked to something new—the view.

Before me the ocean was sparkling like a diamond. Several sailboats were anchored in a straight line fifty feet beyond the wharf and one or two people were swimming in the water. Directly below me some kids were renting plastic yellow paddle boats and I watched as they paddled up Soquel Creek that feeds here into the ocean. Lost in the sights I didn't notice the smoker who had come out on deck to light up. The stream of tobacco smoke took me by surprise and I liked what I was smelling. "Oh god," I said to myself, "will I ever go back to smoking?" It would be very embarrassing to have written all this and then go back.

"She sure tried anyway!"

But this will probably never happen. Not that there isn't a problem. There is. Now I'm addicted to espressos. Actually it's worse than this. I'm addicted to the cafe I write them in. Where once I couldn't write without a cigarette going now I can't write without a whole cafe going. I want the clacking of coffee cups being washed in the sink. I need the clashing of silverware being thrown into the drying basket. I crave Mozart on the stereo competing with the whistling espresso machine. I can't live without the sea of conversation all around me, the cash register ringing, Morris the cat, the waitresses, the regulars, the cheerfulness every morning. How, oh how, am I *ever* going to lose my addiction to all this?

About the Author

Cynthia Morgan attended San Jose State University where she majored in literature. Afterwards she went on to a not-so-highbrow career as a caretaker. Both she and her nineteen-year-old daughter, Sybil, a prominent character in this book, live in Santa Cruz, California. Cynthia is now working on a novel about a contemporary female outlaw.

Footnotes

CHAPTER THREE

1. Fisher, Robert L. *The Odyssey of Tobacco.* (Connecticut: The Prospect Press, 1939), 4–5.
2. Ibid., 19.
3. Apperson, G.L. *The Social History of Smoking.* (London: Martin Secker, 1914), 77.
4. Ibid., 77.
5. Bain, John. *Tobacco.* (New York: H.M. Calwell Co., 1896), 8–9.
6. Lehman Brothers. *All About Tobacco.* (Lehman Brothers, 1955), 11.
7. Dunhill, Alfred D. *The Gentle Art of Smoking.* (London: Max Reinhardt, 1954), 1.
8. Ibid., 9–10.

CHAPTER FIVE

1. Corti, Count. *A History of Smoking.* (London: George G. Harrap & Co. Ltd., 1931), 135.
2. Ibid., 141.
3. *Cope's Mixture: Pipes and Meerschaum*/Part 1. (Liverpool: At the Office of *"Cope's Tobacco Plant." 1893),* 20.
4. Ibid.,22.
5. Sobel, Robert. *They Satisfy: The Cigarette in American Life.* (New York: Anchor Press/Doubleday, 1978), 87.

CHAPTER SIX

1. Meerlo, Joost A. *Suicide and Mass Suicide.* (New York: E.P. Dutton & Co. Inc., 1962), 72–73.

CHAPTER EIGHT

1. Sobel, Robert. *They Satisfy: The Cigarette in American Life.* (New York: Anchor Press/Doubleday, 1978), 103.
2. "George Washington Hill Dies," *Life*, September 23, 1946.
3. Sobel, Robert. *They Satisfy: The Cigarette in American Life.* (New York: Anchor Press/Doubleday, 1978),103.
4. Flynn, John T. "Edward L. Bernays: The Science of Ballyhoo," *The Atlantic Monthly*, May 1932, 562–71.
5. Rowsome, Frank, Jr. *They Laughed When I Sat Down: An informal history of advertising in words and pictures.* (New York: Bonanza Books, 1959), 99.
6. Marchande, Roland. *Advertising the American Dream.* (Berkeley and Los Angeles: University of California Press, 1985), 357–58.
7. Apperson, G.L. *The Social History of Smoking.* (London: The Ballantine Press, 1914), 214–15.
8. Ibid., 218–19.
9. Sobel, Robert. *They Satisfy: The Cigarette in American Life.* (New York: Anchor Press/Doubleday, 1978), 95.

10. Ibid., 95.
11. *Saturday Evening Post*, January 19, 1929, 97.
12. Sobel, Robert. *They Satisfy: The Cigarette in American Life*. (New York: Anchor Press/Doubleday, 1978), 109.
13. "Cigarette Makers Invoke Law to Impede 'Rolling-Your-Own,'" *Business Week*, October 28, 1931, 14.
14. *Newsweek*, March 11, 1940, 56.
15. Sobel, Robert. *They Satisfy: The Cigarette in American Life*. (New York: Anchor Press/Doubleday, 1978), 131.
16. "The Age of the Cigarette," *Time*, January 13, 1947.
17. Ibid.

CHAPTER TEN
1. Marchande, Roland. *Advertising the American Dream*. (Berkeley and Los Angeles: University of California Press, 1985), 275.
2. Ibid., 358.
3. *American Magazine*, July, 1926, 135.
4. Sobel, Robert. *They Satisfy: The Cigarette in American Life*. (New York: Anchor Press/Doubleday, 1978), 176.

CHAPTER ELEVEN
1. Infante, Cabrera. *Holy Smoke*. (London: Faber and Faber Limited, 1985), 99.
2. Ibid., 98.
3. Ibid., 89.

CHAPTER THIRTEEN
1. Geisinger, David L. *Kicking It: The New Way to Stop Smoking Permanently*. (New York: Grove Press, Inc., 1978), 75–78.

CHAPTER FOURTEEN
1. Corti, Count. *A History of Smoking*. (London: George G. Harrap & Co. Ltd., 1931), 233.
2. Dunhill, Alfred D. *The Gentle Art of Smoking*. (London: Max Reinhardt, 1954), 118–119.
3. Sobel, Robert. *They Satisfy: The Cigarette in American Life*. (New York: Anchor Press/Doubleday, 1978), 67–70.

CHAPTER FIFTEEN
1. Infante, Cabrera, *Holy Smoke*. (London: Faber and Faber Limited, 1985), 64.

CHAPTER SIXTEEN
1. Cummins, Ken. "The Cigarette Makers: How They Get Away With Murder," *Washington Monthly*, April 11, 1984, 22.
2. Ibid., 22.
3. Marchande, Roland. *Advertising the American Dream*. (Berkeley and Los Angeles: University of California Press, 1985), 97.
4. Ibid., 99–100.

CHAPTER SEVENTEEN

1. Sobel, Robert. *They Satisfy: The Cigarette in American Life.* (New York: Anchor Press/Doubleday, 1978), 213.
2. Cummins, Ken, "The Cigarette Makers: How They Get Away With Murder," *Washington Monthly*, April, 1984, 25.
3. Babyak, Blythe, "Califano's Cigarette Campaign: all smoke and no fire," *Washington Monthly*, July, 1978, 32–6.
4. "Still Puffing, Joe?" *New Republic*, January 28, 1978, 10.
5. Ibid.
6. Babyak, Blythe, "Califano's Cigarette Campaign: all smoke and no fire," *Washington Monthly*, July, 1978, 32–6.
7. Geisinger, David L. *Kicking It: The New Way to Stop Smoking Permanently.* (New York: Grove Press, Inc., 1978), 172–175
8. Cummins, Ken, "The Cigarette Makers: How They Get Away With Murder," *Washington Monthly*, April, 1984, 24.
9. "Puffing Up the Ritz," *Time*, February 4, 1985, 46.
10. Sobel, Robert. *They Satisfy: The Cigarette in American Life.* (New York: Anchor Press/Doubleday, 1978), 207–9.
11. Ibid.
12. Sources for Newspaper Headlines on page 119
    a. Survey finds 18 million join in Great American Smokeout, New York Times–November 16, 1984.
    b. Move toward a "smoke free" US gains steadily. Christian Science Monitor-June 18, 1986.
    c. Singapore sets sights on "smoke-free" goal; Christian Science Monitor, January 21, 1987.
    d. Jersey seeks tighter curbs on smoking. New York Times, November 23 1986.
    e. The most addictive drug. (Nancy Reagan should attack tobacco smoking). (column) by Ellen Goodman, Washington Post, December 12, 1985.
    f. Lung cancer is expected to become top killer of women. New York Times, January 16, 1985.
    g. Harmful habit; cigarette smoking is growing hazardous to careers in business; . . . Wall Street Journal, April 23, 1987.
13. Smokers have rights, too. (column) by Ernest van den Haag, New York Times, April 9, 1985.

Bibliography

Apperson, G.L. *The Social History of Smoking*. (London: Martin Secker, 1914).

Bain, John. *Tobacco*. (New York: H.M. Calwell Co., 1896).

Cope's Mixture: Pipes and Meerschaum/Part 1. (Liverpool: At the Office of "Cope's Tobacco Plant," 1893).

Corti, Count. *A History of Smoking*. (London: George G. Harrap & Co. Ltd., 1931).

Dunhill, Alfred D. *The Gentle Art of Smoking*. (London: Max Reinhardt, 1954).

Fisher, Robert L. *The Odyssey of Tobacco*. (Connecticut: The Prospect Press, 1939).

Geisinger, David L. *Kicking It: The New Way to Stop Smoking Permanently*. (New York: Grove Press, Inc., 1978).

Infante, Cabrera. *Holy Smoke*. (London: Faber and Faber Limited, 1985).

Kanin, Garson. *Hollywood*. (New York: The Viking Press, Inc., 1974).

Lehman Brothers. *All About Tobacco*. (Lehman Brothers, 1955).

Marchande, Roland. *Advertising the American Dream*. (Berkeley and Los Angeles: University of California Press, 1985).

Meerlo, Joost A. *Suicide and Mass Suicide*. (New York: E.P. Dutton & Co. Inc., 1962).

Rowsome, Frank, Jr. *They Laughed When I Sat Down: An informal history of advertising in words and pictures*. (New York: Bonanza Books, 1959).

Sobel, Robert. *They Satisfy: The Cigarette in American Life*. (New York: Anchor Press/Doubleday, 1978).